JESUS AND THE

WOMEN OF THE BIBLE

CHIDERAH COX

Published by Monde Global Press
Author website: www.chiderahcox.com

Cover Design by Bayo Dare, www.bayodare.com
Edited by Natalie Lowell, www.exquisitepage.com

ISBN: 979-8-9950574-0-6 (paperback)

ACKNOWLEDGMENTS

Grateful acknowledgement is given to my mother, Dr. Vera Monde-Anumihe, the first and best example of godly womanhood that I've known and admired;

To my father, Nkem Monde-Anumihe, PhD, for teaching me how to meditate on the Word and search the Scriptures;

To my sisters, Adanna and Chinenye, who stand beside me as beautiful and powerful women of God;

To my sister-friends Ogechi Umeh, Zaneta Forson-Dare, and Kelly Tchemi, whose review of this book and thought-provoking conversations have strengthened my faith;

To Lisa Coffman, and all of the ladies who participated in the *Jesus and the Women of the Bible* study groups at Catalyst Church;

To my editor Natalie Lowell and designer Bayo Dare for your work on this book;

To Emmanuel and Elisha, who have changed my life for the better with the precious gift of motherhood;

To Austin and Cora, with whom I'm learning how to nurture in new ways;

And to Ryan, my husband, whose support and partnership frees me to be the woman that God created me to be—

Thank you.

For Cora

JESUS
AND THE

WOMEN
OF THE BIBLE

CONTENTS

This book aims to explore the Biblical characteristics of womanhood that define the collective experience of women and reflect the heart of God.

We should learn from the women of the Bible because each of their lives and stories tell us something important about who God is, and how He intended for women to live.

By God's design, women have purpose, strength, resolve, wisdom, and beauty.

In Him, women have all of the agency, authority, permission and power that they need.

INTRODUCTION

When you first open the box for an appliance you purchased, you expect to find a manual. Whether it's a booklet or folded piece of paper full of instructions, most everyday household items, from kids' toys to coffee makers, come with a guide for how to use the item and how to put it together. There are details about various features and functions, where the power button is, the different settings for use, and who to contact when something isn't working the way it should. Perhaps most important, in every manual there are instructions about what *not to do* with your new item. These instruction manuals typically include a mailing address or customer support phone number, so you know exactly where to send your complaint or return the item for a refund. And sometimes the manual includes a warranty, which promises that the creator will fix or replace your item if it malfunctions. Some warranties are bound by a timeframe, while others are for a lifetime. Every created thing seems to come with a manual or guide for use from its creator. And humans are no exception.

It might sound like an oversimplification to call the Bible our instruction manual for life, but in a lot of ways it is. In this great big book of inspired words are explanations, instructions, and even warranties in the form of promises that lead us straight to the heart of our Creator, God. So here we find the same concept; in the Bible there are specifications for human design. It explains our origins and behaviors, and it gives us direction for our lives and how to exist on earth. In the Bible there are stories that show us how to interact with others, and some of these stories tell us what not to do. Most importantly, with the example of Jesus, the Bible tells us who to contact when something isn't working the way it should.

The Bible is a book about humans interacting with the God who created them for His own pleasure. We exist to give God glory by worshipping Him with our entire beings; in fact we were created for this sole purpose as image-bearers, operating as extensions and reflections of Him on the earth. While we don't know the exact thoughts of the Creator or exactly *why* He created us for this purpose, through the lives and circumstances of people in the Bible we are able to learn a little about the character, heart, and nature of God. Through the stories and experiences of men and women in the Bible, we are able to see God's design and intentions for His creation, with His sovereignty and providence over their lives, and His guidance in their affairs.

Everything in the Bible points to Jesus. Through the progression of events, which spans several hundreds of years of human history recorded in 66 books, we're able to see God's ultimate plan of redemption come to fruition through our Savior, Jesus Christ. But what do we do with everyone else in the book? The hundreds of names and hundreds of stories are included in this helpful guide for a reason. Many of the most famous and widely circulated stories from the Bible involve men of courage, stature and nobility, such as David, Moses, Joseph, and Daniel, all of whom we can learn from and aspire to be like. Many other stories tell us of the prophets of God, like Elijah, Samuel, or Jonah, and through their many adventures we see how God delivered messages of faith and assurance to His people who needed direction in times of trouble. Still others, like Matthew, Peter, and Paul, expand our knowledge of God as they present the teachings of Jesus and His ways after their encounters with Him, focusing our attention on how to maintain fervent faith after Jesus's departure from the earth. All of these men are great examples for all of us. But, so are the women.

In modern society, and most obviously since the middle of the 20th century in America and many other cultures, there appears to be much confusion about what a woman is. A woman's inherent design and God-given purpose has been called into question, even outwardly rejected, while her reproductive role has been the subject of endless debate. The influence of the feminist movement has permeated every sphere of the modern woman's life, and the result is that the very things women were created by God to do – including things we could easily identify like marriage and childbirth – are now rejected by many women, usurped by men, or simply seen as archaic, unimportant, or undesirable for a modern-day lifestyle.

The truth is that every woman was created to be a helpmate and a nurturer. And every woman was created to have dominion. We read this in the book of Genesis: to help produce and to nurture, or provide care, in whatever dominion God gives us, is the tangible work of a woman. Women are uniquely and intricately designed by God, and full of beauty, grace, and wisdom that enable them to be the perfect helpmates. The work of the woman within the marriage union is the same work of the Church, called the Bride of Christ. The Bride is called to have dominion, to help, and to nurture humanity in order to facilitate the perfect work of our Savior, the Bridegroom, Jesus Christ, on the earth and in each person's heart.

Today, we've forgotten the significance of this important role. You see, the crisis of biblical womanhood goes far beyond discussions of gender norms and reproductive rights; it is far beyond vocation or school or lifestyle choices. The devil is committed to destroying the very identity of a woman as an image-bearer of God and as a reflection of the Bride of Christ. We are joint heirs who are destined to reign with Jesus Christ. The devil knows that if he can keep us from *that* truth, then he can destroy our understanding of our position and inheritance as sons and daughters of the Most High God.

I'll take it a step further and say that if women are confused about womanhood, then women are confused about who God is. The devil's goal here is to delay his inevitable demise. To that end, he causes as much confusion as he can in humanity. He wants to take as many image-bearers as possible to hell with him when he perishes. Many women don't know their purpose or God's heart for womanhood, and in turn, this ignorance leads to our devaluation. When women devalue themselves, they forfeit their true power and authority.

This, of course, is not a surprise to God. And all hope is not lost. As women, we must remember the identity we already have in Christ. The decline of society's understanding of the purpose of women has been a slow one, but not an undocumented one. We have centuries of records of women in the Bible who emulated the characteristics of God and who lived out His design and intent for womanhood in their interactions with other people, before and after Jesus walked the earth. But the narratives and stories about women in relation to God are rarely taught from the pulpit.

Contrary to any belief that a woman is somehow less valued by God or that Eve was created only to serve Adam, the Hebrew translation of "helpmate," which is "ezer kenegdo" according to the Torah (Rendsburg, 2021), actually suggests a position of power and equality. This translation tells us something very important about God. It demonstrates that He intended for the woman to equally represent His nature and essence alongside the man, with the two of them completing His image and furthering His will and work in the world. It also suggests that God intended for the woman to do something important—she was not created to be idle. Together, man and woman have an assignment, a dominion mandate, that requires their individual contributions and partnership to complete.

Unique characteristics of God's Spirit are reflected and highlighted in the woman's being; for example, women are fruitful, given the ability to bring forth life in childbirth, just as the Spirit gives life. Women are compassionate and caring, reflected in the ability to nurture. The woman's fruitfulness is not restricted to childbearing; she is a producer in various capacities, whether at home or at work. She reflects the beauty of God, and she has an innate desire to see beauty in her environments. Women are also intuitive, which reflects a God-given gift of discernment.

There are over 150 women named in the Bible, each with a unique place in God's story. So, where do we start? At the beginning, of course. We have the very first woman, Eve, spoken into existence by God Himself, created as an important consideration for Adam's wellbeing. Eve's flaws are on display for us to learn from as we read the story of her life in Genesis, alongside examples of her beauty, her strength, her wisdom, her sadness, and most importantly, her relationships with God and Adam. After Eve, we get the full spectrum of the female experience in the women of the Bible; women who were mothers, daughters, married, single, rich, poor, young, and old. Women whose prophecies moved nations to action. Women who enriched their communities with the work of their hands. Women who were wicked, cruel, jealous, and manipulative. Women who were wise, enterprising, confident and brave. Women whose tears of pain and joy were poured out as praises to God. Women who Jesus encountered directly and profoundly, and women who were in the periphery of society, as slaves or concubines. Some were queens; others were nameless. But they're all in the Book.

We begin our study of the women of the Bible by learning from thirteen of them - Eve, Sarah and Hagar, Rachel and Leah, Rahab, Ruth and Naomi, Esther, Bathsheba, Mary and Martha of Bethany, and the Woman at the Well. These women are incredible examples of faith, courage, wisdom, and redemption. None of them are perfect, but all of them put their trust in God. Through their stories and His divine interactions with them, we can begin to gain deeper insights into God's purpose for our womanhood today, and His heart and will for all women throughout all generations. By looking at their lives as an example, we can discover how the women of the Bible reflect the nature of God, and the grace, truth, and salvation found in our Savior Jesus Christ.

The Old Testament shows us many examples of women who were exalted to positions of leadership, status, or prominence by God Himself. Prophetesses such as Miriam and Huldah, queens like Esther and Bathsheba, and even pagans like Rahab and Ruth were divinely positioned by God for leadership and impact. Their lives were catalysts of change, either for the continuation of the nation of Israel or for the coming of its King, Jesus.

In Bible stories with female heroines, the women come alongside men of God to carry out their assignments, emphasizing the partnership between the two sexes. But there are also times when the Lord sets women apart. There are instances, such as with Deborah or Esther, when God places women in positions of leadership and authority in times of war and conflict, entrusting them to bear witness to His will and reveal His plans to kings and military leaders.

We see in several other examples that God amplifies a woman's purpose, beauty, and strength in the midst of her rejection, shame, or pain. Although Bathsheba was eventually elevated to queendom, she endured hardship and experienced loneliness and sorrow in the palace. God's favor rests with her, and her womanhood is honored. Similarly, while women like Leah and Hagar were rejected by the men in their lives, they were chosen and called worthy to bring forth nations by God. He determined their value, not men.

The point of this book is to illustrate that the women in the Bible have lives that look a lot like ours, and that is not by coincidence. Their lives should be studied in order for us to understand what womanhood really is. These women made mistakes, were susceptible to the influences of their societies and cultures, and had personal insecurities and fears. Through their stories, their triumphs, and mishaps, we have an opportunity to understand what God says about them that can also be said about us today.

To bring back the analogy of the Bible as a life manual - just like any other handy guide, in order to understand the design of a created thing, or even be reminded that there is a design, we have to refer back to the owner's manual. This book is not a replacement for the Bible. It should serve as a companion to reading the scriptures. We will take the Word at face value, reading the stories of each woman to extrapolate and analyze her character, interactions, responses, and experiences. It will be necessary to consider the historical context and culture that each woman lives in, and overall, we will see that their womanhood is the same as ours today.

Womanhood, in its fullness, glorifies God. We have to be able to see the uniqueness of the woman, knowing that God put as much of Himself into creating the woman as He did with the man. We should celebrate that God designed her in His image and set her on earth and in time with purpose, with certain attributes that reflect His nature. Unless we acknowledge God's masterful handiwork, our view of women will be distorted.

JESUS AND...

Make no mistake, this is a book about Jesus. If in the beginning was the Word, and the Word was God (John 1:1), and the Word gave life to creation and is ever-present in it, then His presence is in every story. Every woman in the Bible has a story that points back to Jesus, whether it's through her character, her faith, or her direct interactions with Him. In every instance of a woman redeemed, Jesus is represented. He is the scarlet rope (Joshua 2:21), the birthed child (Genesis 21:1), and the victory over evil men (Esther 7:6-8). When a woman's prayer is answered, Jesus is the one interceding on her behalf. He caught her tears of sorrow (1 Samuel 1:7); He comforted her in the wilderness (Genesis 21:14-19); He gave her a song of praise (Luke 1:46-55); He changed her life forever (Luke 8:2). His faithfulness towards women has endured for generations. His promises to women are yes and amen. His loving-kindness towards women is evident in every triumph of their strength and will.

Jesus, being the full expression of God in the flesh, demonstrates many of the characteristics and personality traits that God gives to women, even while walking in His complete manhood as the bride-groom to the Church. He is compassionate and caring, reflecting the concern for others that women are called to emulate. He nurtures and teaches. As the ultimate helpmate to humanity, He exudes wisdom and grace, and His life is an example of the call to servanthood and submission. Godly women look like Him.

In many of His New Testament encounters, Jesus takes a counter-cultural approach to his relationships with women, seeing and speaking to them as equal to men and allowing them to have agency and authority to demonstrate their faith in Him. Jesus honored His mother's wishes at the wedding of Cana, performing His first miracle at her request despite initially saying it wasn't yet His time (John 2:3-4). He considered Martha and Mary dear friends whose home He would visit and whose act of worship He would celebrate (Luke 10:38-42). Jesus spoke to the woman caught in the act of adultery with compassion and care, stepping between her and the group of men ready to throw stones (John 8:1-11). He addressed the Samaritan woman at the well at a time and in a manner that no other Jewish man would find acceptable (John 4:1-42). His ministry was funded and supported by wealthy women like Joanna and Susanna. His wise counsel included women disciples like Mary Magdalene. In fact, Jesus chose to reveal His risen self to Mary and Joanna before he went to see any of His other disciples. And after His time on earth was done, women like Priscilla and Lydia were instrumental in furthering His Kingdom message. We see Jesus had no problem with women who used the work of their hands to advance the will of God.

Early Christian church leaders like Paul and Peter modeled the same Christ-like appreciation for women by working alongside them in ministry. Paul greets at least eighteen women of faith who led churches or ministries in his letters (Schnorr, 2024), including Priscilla, Phoebe, Junia, Tryphaena, and Tryphosa, mentioned in Romans 16. Likewise, during his travels, Peter makes an important stop in Joppa to visit and resurrect Tabitha, a respected Christian woman and disciple of Jesus (Acts 9:38). Luke's gospel prominently features divine encounters involving women, including Mary, mother of Jesus, and Elizabeth (Luke 1), Anna (Luke 2:36-38) and Simon's mother-in-law (Luke 4:38-39).

Jesus's view of women aligns perfectly with His Father's will and purpose for them from the very beginning as equally important facilitators of the Kingdom. And God is unchanging. If He placed that much value on women back then, He certainly values women now.

EVE

Read: Genesis 1-3

If you were offered the chance to be like God, would you take it?

Eve is the most famous representation of a woman, as she shows us all that being a woman encompasses. After all, her name means "mother of all who have life." She is the essence, the origin, the representation of motherhood and womanhood —Eve's story is every woman's story.

Eve was the completion of God's good and perfect creation. In the Genesis story, after He created the heavens and the earth, the land and the waters, the animals and the birds and called all of those things *good*, God made two beings in his image as the last stop of creation. Adam was fashioned from the dust of the earth first, but after giving the man a purpose and assigning him a task, God noticed that something about this creature's existence was *not good*: his aloneness (Genesis 2:18). Thus, God made Eve to solve this problem, giving the man the help and companionship he needed (Genesis 2:20). God came up with the idea to take a rib from the man to create the second being, which Adam later called woman (Genesis 2:23). The Scripture says that none of the livestock, birds, nor wild animals could be what Adam needed. Nothing else, in all of creation, helps a man achieve his destiny like a woman can. The two of them, man and woman together, reflect God's relational nature. In the middle of the story, the writer of Genesis also explains in an aside that this is the intent of marriage (Genesis 2:24).

"This explains why a man leaves his father and mother and is joined to his wife, and the two are united into one."

The marriage union, when done correctly, is a reflection of God; it is a reflection of Jesus Christ and His Church-bride. As an individual, Eve represents something unique about God. She was created with certain characteristics of His nature that could not be given to man or to the animals. In other words, she brought something new to the world. We certainly see the difference between man and woman in anatomical parts, and we have been taught about each gender based on what society believes about their roles and behaviors. But Eve's creation is different than Adam's because the woman reflects God's life-giving and nurturing care. She embodies attentiveness, gentleness, and partnership with man in ways that mirror God's own character. These attributes enable a woman to fulfill her God-given purpose alongside man to steward creation, have dominion, and participate in God's mandate to be fruitful and multiply, extending into future generations. While Adam's purpose was to work (Genesis 2:15), cultivating the earth through the leadership and stewardship of their dominion, God decided that the man could not achieve the heights of his intended purpose and design by himself. He needed a woman.

Eve is the reason that women love as hard, fight as hard, and hurt as hard as we do. We blame her for our "woman problems," for the pain associated with menstrual cycles, emotional ups and downs, and absolutely everything involving pregnancy. Every once in a while, women sigh a weary sigh and think, *thanks Eve*. It may sound like a lot to put on the shoulders of one woman, but those lofty accusations are fitting for the level of seriousness of Eve's sin. Think about the Creation story that you know. It probably focuses on the first two humans being happy and content in the Garden of Eden, until they ate a fruit that they were told not to eat, and as a result were punished by God. A lot of attention is given to Adam and Eve's actions in that story, but not what led to them. Those details are equally, if not more important.

God's punishment for the naked human couple may seem severe. After all, Eve is kicked out of God's presence, prescribed pain in childbearing, and given what can be described as a lifetime of unfulfillment and submission in her partnership with Adam. But what if I told you that by her actions, Eve was behaving just like the devil. She was subtly prideful, which we see through the encounter she has with the serpent, and she wanted something that God had: infinite wisdom. She wanted to be just like God.

"She saw that the tree was beautiful and its fruit looked delicious, and she wanted the wisdom it would give her." (Genesis 3:6)

Let's break this down. Before the encounter with the serpent, and before the woman was "convinced" by his words, her only reference for wisdom was God. The Lord provided everything she and Adam needed, and He always told them what to do. The fruit offered a likeness to God that she thought would give her more freedom than she already had in Him. The serpent told the woman that eating the fruit would make her like God. That aspiration to *be* like God was what convinced her to take the bite. It may not have been a new idea the serpent was introducing; his words likely confirmed a thought Eve already pondered and perhaps stored in her heart. A contemplation, or a daydream, in which she imagined a God-like existence—

making her own decisions and exploring the newly created world in her own way, without the oversight. This was a dream worth risking it all by eating the fruit. And this was the pride that brewed deep in Eve's heart. She slowly accepted the thought that the serpent was there to confirm—one that told her, *you could be like God.*

But what Eve failed to realize was that she was already like God. In fact, she was made perfect in Him. So Eve's next sin was rejecting the truth of who God created her to be, and thus, denying the truth of who He is. God does not make mistakes. He created Eve as perfectly as she could have been—lacking nothing, with the capacity to depend fully on Him. But her free will, which God also gave her, led her wildly astray. Eve exhibits a lack of trust in God, which is another very serious offense. Let's pause to let this marinate. Do you see how we often make the same mistake?

Another sin you may not have noticed from this origin story is Eve's distance from the Word of God. Back then, Eve didn't have a guide like the Bible to refer to, but we know the Word of God *was there* in the beginning—and there were actual words that God spoke directly to Adam. Eve is able to be swayed by the devil's proposition in part because she had prideful thoughts of her own grandeur, and in part because she did not receive God's Word after hearing it from Adam. The battle is already lost by the time she is ready to eat the apple. When the devil asks if God *really* said not to eat the fruit, Eve replies:

"God said, 'You must not eat it or even touch it; if you do, you will die'" (Genesis 3:3).

But that is not exactly how He said it. In Genesis 2, God gives Adam a very simple word of caution:

"You may freely eat the fruit of every tree in the garden— except the tree of the knowledge of good and evil. If you eat its fruit, you are sure to die" (Genesis 2:16-17).

Notice the difference in tone? Somehow Eve has a much harsher interpretation of God's Word, which begs the question of how Adam was communicating to his wife about God. Perhaps Eve misunderstood God's command to be a harsh restriction rather than a loving caution for her benefit because she didn't know His voice as well as her husband. Speaking of Adam, many people believe that Eve sinned alone by listening to the serpent, biting the apple and giving it to him afterwards, but Adam was right next to her. There's a lot to be said about the man's responsibility in all of this, and the fact that Adam was the one who received the command from God, not Eve. Somehow, even if Adam paraphrased what God said when he told his wife, Eve hears a voice of rebuke rather than the words of a loving Father. God gave Adam and Eve a safeguard from death, but they received it as a limit on their freedom.

In comparison to Eve's conversation with the serpent, we can look at the stark difference in Jesus's posture when confronted with the devil's temptations in the wilderness as recorded in the Gospels of Matthew, Mark and Luke. Jesus's immediate response to the devil's proposals is to rebuke him with the Word of God. He does not give the devil's lies and promises of a better life the chance to settle into his mind. In fact, Jesus was so sure about God's Word that He could not be persuaded into believing that there was a better way. Nothing the devil could say would be more true than what Jesus knew about God. Eve couldn't say the same, even despite living in God's company. It's important to know God's Word just as Jesus did in that moment so we don't allow any room for doubt, because we know that God is faithful to His Word.

From this brief first encounter with Eve, we also get to see the devil's true nature for the first time. He is the same in all of the stories throughout the Bible. The enemy always comes with deception through lies, twisting the Word of God to suit the situation, or looking for doubt in our minds and space in our relationship with God. In one mouthful of words (Genesis

3:4-5), the devil comes against God's truth by saying Eve would not die; then he manipulates the intent of God's command to be forbidding rather than loving, while causing the pride in Eve's heart to rise. The woman falls from grace in her heart the same way the devil did, and just as quickly discovers the repercussions of sin. In Eve's story, we see Satan in his first successful attempt at making sure that God's creation would suffer the same fate he is destined to have. As they say, misery loves company.

Eve saw that the tree was beautiful and its fruit looked delicious, and she ate it; then she gave some to her husband who was with her (Genesis 3:6). The sequence in this passage shows that Eve inherited sinful behaviors almost instantly. In a matter of moments she grows in lust, covetousness, greed, and gluttony as soon as her prideful thoughts allow her to be convinced by the serpent. By eating the fruit, Adam and Eve's "eyes were opened" (Genesis 3:7). They received knowledge first, but the next thing they feel is shame. Here's the part that sticks out to me: if the first thing that the man and woman feel after eating the fruit is shame, which is a direct result of sin, it means that everything they had before they ate the fruit—was good. Not sin. Everything that God had given Eve so far in her life was the best that they could have ever had. How did she not see that? Eve had communion with God and basked in the fruits of the Spirit. In Eden she had love, joy, peace, and every other good and perfect thing. God said *it was good* after each day of His creation. So if Eve already had it good, how did she not remember all of the goodness in her life when talking to the devil? By not being focused on God. By not seeking His counsel when a new influence entered her life; by not taking a moment to pause and ask Him, *is this serpent good?* By not staying close to God; by not knowing His voice so well that any other voice that didn't sound like Him wouldn't have had the opportunity to sway her thinking.

In another tragic consequence of this fateful exchange, Eve compromises her identity as a woman. By engaging with the serpent and eating the fruit, Eve abandons her God-given responsibility to be Adam's helpmate. In doing so, she jeopardizes his identity as well. We see that Eve steers the man away from God by giving him the fruit. It is not a coincidence that the serpent approaches the woman and not the man first; he knows that if he can affect her, she will influence him. We see the enemy's manipulative tactics in Eve's story, and in other instances in the Bible where sinful women negatively influence their men, including Delilah, Jezebel, Potiphar's Wife, and Herodias. If we really stop to think about it, we still see this same toxic dynamic play out in modern society. Throughout history, in culture, in relationships, and in work, a woman is often a man's biggest influence, for better or for worse.

Perhaps Adam could have corrected Eve's misinterpretation of God's words. Maybe he could have rebuked the devil himself at that moment in the garden. While Eve is being introduced to the consequences of sin, Adam is right there, abandoning his responsibilities as a husband and leader. Even if he didn't rebuke Eve in the moment, Adam could have left the woman to make the mistake alone and run back to God for help. Instead, he was also convinced by the serpent, but then blamed Eve (Genesis 3:12).

There is a brand of feminism today that would have us women believe that men are our biggest problem. They say that men are inherently bad for us, and that in today's scientific world, Eve doesn't actually need an Adam—not even for reproduction. This feminism has a long, rich history to draw from, ripe with examples of oppression of women at the hands of evil men. There are valid examples; we know that women all over the world and throughout history have suffered, often beyond comprehension, at the hands of evil men. And some women around the world still suffer, with gender-based violence, misogyny, religious oppression, and exclusion from basic rights rampant in various patriarchal societies. But, while evil men certainly do exist, and there are more than enough examples of their atrocities to make a case against men, these heinous acts are not a reflection of the God-given nature of man. Evil men are a reflection of the nature of evil. Everything bad about an evil man can be attributed to the evil within the man's heart. It's a subtle, but poignant distinction to make, and one that requires a weighty shift in perspective to see the truth —but it is true. And once you see it, you see that the battle is not with man; it is with evil. That's exactly what God said would happen (Genesis 3:15). Our biggest battle as women, despite what we see every day, is believing that the serpent, not the man, is our enemy.

The greatest honor given to Eve by God was the ability to bring life into the world through childbearing. As a consequence of her actions, this honor would now require Eve to endure what many know to be the greatest physical pain humanly possible in labor. In her relationship with Adam, and the abandonment of her purpose to help, Eve is sentenced to a lifetime of submission and unmatched desire. With the knowledge of evil now within her, the woman inherits a lifetime of pain, shame, and sorrow. We know these emotions all too well today, but rarely do we equate them with the consequences of sin.

In the end, Eve unknowingly gives the devil access to her soul. Her mind, her will, and her emotions become corrupted as evil permeates to her heart. All of us are equally vulnerable and susceptible to the all-consuming desire for the things of the world, crippling insecurity in our identity, and stagnancy in our relationships with God. We can easily find ourselves doubting God, not trusting His sovereignty, and not believing that His commands are given for our good. We can see them as limits too. Just like Eve, we leave Eden behind, taking others out with us, and sometimes with generational effect.

God remains merciful, faithful, and kind to Eve. Even after the betrayal, He takes the position of love and blesses the human couple with a lifetime of opportunities to stay close to Him. God immediately provides clothes for their shame

(Genesis 3:21). And although He has to banish them from the garden, He never leaves them. Instead, our God draws nearer to Adam and Eve, and He goes with them to fulfill His plan of redeeming creation from that moment forward.

God knew the end, even at the beginning. He punished the serpent, making sure that we would never benefit from a relationship with evil, and that the forces and spirits warring against humanity would submit to our authority in the name of Jesus Christ. Eve's story sets the stage for this epic battle. God said that there would be enmity between the serpent and the woman's offspring; that he would bruise the serpent's head, and the serpent would bruise his heel (Genesis 3:15). With Jesus's death, Satan thought he had won, but it was only a heel strike causing temporary pain. With the resurrection, Jesus won with a fatal strike to the head of evil, just as God said it would be in the beginning. And as for Eve, she would be redeemed by her offspring, referring to her descendant, Jesus Christ. Eve's salvation came the same way ours does today—only through Jesus.

THE WOMANHOOD OF EVE

Eve represents companionship, beauty, and the nurturing spirit of motherhood. She is helpful, gentle, and caring, and has a position of influence in Adam's life as his God-ordained partner. But Eve also possesses pride and selfish ambition, and she exhibits a lack of discernment by her actions in the Genesis story. She introduces control and manipulation in her ability to persuade Adam; and in her conviction to eat the fruit, we see deep-rooted vanity and gluttony. Nonetheless, we know that Eve perseveres. God uses Eve for His life-giving purposes through childbearing, which is a reflection and foreshadowing of the life-giving salvation we receive through Jesus. We know that this process requires significant pain and significant sacrifice. God chooses Eve to be strong enough to endure. Eve's story is the first example of God's steadfast love, grace, mercy, and faithfulness, and her story shows His redemptive plan for women from the very beginning of time.

Take a moment to reflect on Eve's womanhood:

What similarities do you see to your own?

What character flaws does she demonstrate, and what are her redemptive qualities?

Write down your biggest takeaway about God from Eve's story below:

SARAH & HAGAR

Read: Genesis 12-21

Have you ever stopped to wonder if, perhaps, you might be the cause of your own problems?

The story of Sarah is one that requires a lot of grace to understand from a woman's perspective. In a moment of disbelieving laughter she doubted God's plan, but He still gave her the title of "mother of many nations" (Genesis 17:17) and blessed her with the promised child Isaac. Why? Because God's miraculous power and sovereignty would be on full display through her life despite her doubt. His promises to Abraham would come to pass, and Sarah's story proves that even when we create our own chaos and confusion, the truth of God's faithfulness remains.

Sarah is the only woman known in the Bible to have given birth at the age of ninety. Such a miraculous event alone would be a shining example of God's sovereignty and unmerited favor in her life, but His faithfulness is seen in many more instances. Her name, Sarah, and her given name Sarai, reflected her level of esteem. Her names translate to "princess" and "woman of high rank" in Hebrew and Arabic, but also mean "quarrelsome," which we learn is true of her character, as evidenced by her fights with Hagar.

Sarai was known as a beautiful, loyal, and devoted wife to Abram. In the land of Haram, her husband was a leader amongst men; Abram was wise, admirable, and successful, boasting land, livestock, gold, and silver (Genesis 13:2). He walked closely with the Lord, who in turn promised that Abram would be blessed and made into a great nation (Genesis 12:2). The only apparent problem with this promise was that Sarai couldn't have children (Genesis 11:30), a reality that she had probably lived with in shame and bitterness for decades by the time we meet her in the story. While Abram received the promise directly from God, Sarai likely wondered if he heard correctly. For Abram, however, having a barren wife did not deter him from accepting God's promise that he would one day have a son and heir (Genesis 15), and the Lord counted him as righteous for his steadfastness in faith.

But Sarai wasn't as patient. While waiting for the promise to be fulfilled, she took matters into her own hands and convinced Abram to sleep with her Egyptian servant Hagar (Genesis 16:2). He took Hagar as a second wife at Sarai's instruction, in order to make God's plan happen sooner rather than later. Sarai devised the plan thinking it would be an arrangement of surrogacy; she would take the child from Hagar and raise him as her own. But she didn't count the cost of this new plan. Sarai didn't consider the possibility that Hagar might not easily give up raising her son. Instead, the servant girl became emboldened by her motherhood. With this new position came new power and authority for Hagar; having a son with Abram meant she had security and a new legacy of nobility. Ishmael was born (Genesis 16:15), and instead of his birth being a time of joy and celebration, it created conflict in the household, with chaos, confusion, and a lot of tension between the two wives.

Reading the scenario, it's easy for us to come to a *well, of course that would go wrong* conclusion. Perhaps you wouldn't resort to those tactics today, but we should also consider the norms of Sarai's society. For a woman in her position, as the wife of a highly respected and rich man, there was likely enormous pressure to maintain her reputation. She cared about her status and how she was perceived by others as a barren wife who couldn't produce an heir for Abram. The promise of a child from God seemed impossible; after all, everyone knew about her age and barrenness. Thus, she acted out of desperation.

To this day, and in many cultures, women are often blamed for infertility. Imagine how much worse it may have been in Sarai's day. It's unclear whether or not the societal pressure was more of a driving factor for Sarai's plan than her desire to produce an heir for Abram's legacy, but it's safe to assume that it must have been equally, if not more important from a social lens. With that, we have to give Sarai some grace. The pressure to maintain status, reputation, and the illusion of a perfect life in the eyes of the public is still a struggle for many women today.

Sarai's doubt becomes more apparent when looking at her situation from a spiritual lens. In this way, her actions become a bit more nuanced and calculated. First, we know that she devised her plan ten years after God moved her and Abram to Canaan (Genesis 16:3), ten years after Abram received God's promise. Ten years is a long time to wait for *anything*, but the wait probably felt longer because Sarai lost sight of the promise. How do we know this? To begin with, God told Abram they would have a child well after Sarai's natural menstrual cycle and birthing years would have ended. She was already in her 60s, and thus the impossibility of the promise alone should have kept her curious and hopeful, ready to receive the miracle in God's due time. This is a test of faith that even women today can fail. If it is already humanly impossible and God says He will do it, then we need to trust His Word and believe that *He will do it.* And while Sarai may not have been outwardly doubting God's supernatural abilities, trying to bring the plan to fruition by herself suggests she had little faith in His promise.

We see that God acknowledged the long wait by sending Abram and Sarai several reassurances while they waited for the promises to be fulfilled. The Scriptures do not specify what year, but we know that some time after giving Abram the initial promise, the Lord speaks to him in a vision (Genesis 15:4), reinforcing that He would give Abram a son of his own to become an heir, this time in direct response to Abram's anxiety about his riches going to a servant.

The Scriptures say that Abram believed the Lord a second time (Genesis 15:6). He executes a sacrifice to ensure God would give him the land, and he receives further revelation about his descendants being oppressed for 400 years in the future (Genesis 15:12-20). We know all of this comes to fruition later with the story of Moses in the book of Exodus, but these clear and specific revelations were enough to assure Abram that God's promise was still on its way. One can't have descendants without at least one child, and God gave him a whole picture of the future.

This is where we have to look at Sarai with a side eye. If Abram told her all of this and explained the revelations he received in great detail, how did she not take it as a sign to relax and just wait? This situation quickly becomes a lesson to all of us. What reassurances from God are we currently dismissing? Whether through His Word, confirmation from another believer, or directly in visions and dreams, God's faithfulness often includes reassurances of the plan He is orchestrating in our lives. We just have to receive them in earnest and continue waiting with patience.

When Hagar became pregnant, the affairs of the household almost immediately turned sour. The servant girl began to treat her mistress with contempt, and Sarai went as far as blaming Abram for the problem *she* created. We then learn that Sarai treated Hagar so harshly that she ran away to the wilderness, where Hagar was met by the Angel of the Lord and told to return and submit. It's easy to sympathize with Hagar at this point. She didn't ask to be included in Sarai's schemes. But despite being told to return to such a toxic environment, we see Hagar still had a humble heart. When the Angel of the Lord asked where she was coming from and going (which is interesting, because He already knew), Hagar responded that she was running from her "mistress" Sarai (Genesis 16:8). She kept her posture of submission. She didn't elevate herself as a mother above Sarai, nor did she add any insult to Sarai's name or slight their relationship. The Lord told her to go back "and submit to her authority" (Genesis 16:9), and she listened.

These words are very carefully spoken by God, showing how much He values order, submission, and humility. It also spoke volumes that Hagar didn't oppose or protest the instruction. Because of her obedience, God let Hagar know that she, too, would have more descendants than she could count (Genesis 16:10). She received the name and promise of Ishmael, and she left the encounter comforted by the fact that God had truly seen her situation (Genesis 16:13). In fact, she named Him El-Roi, meaning "the God who sees me," becoming the first person to give a name to God.

The Angel of the Lord knew exactly where Hagar was, physically, and metaphorically. He met her in the wilderness, the representation of a dark time in her life. God knew what she had gone through with Sarai, and He knew who was right and wrong in the situation. And while God honors authority, He is fair and just. It's His job to fight the battles, and our job to give Him the control. Hagar left the encounter enveloped in His peace and renewed with the hope of His promises. While she knew that she'd be returning to more contention with Sarai, she was now equipped with more reason to endure. Women who are called to endure suffering can take heart from Hagar's example and story. God sees all pain and is near to the brokenhearted. His Word says in 1 Peter 5:10 that "after you have suffered a little while, he will restore, support, and strengthen you, and he will place you on a firm foundation." We see He does exactly that for Hagar.

Eleven years later, when God makes the new covenant changing Abram's name to Abraham and his wife's name to Sarah, the Lord assures, once again, that the promise of an heir is still on the way (Genesis 17:16). This reassurance is even more direct; God actually gives them the name, Isaac (Genesis 17:19), and tells them the baby will be born next year. A t this point Abraham is 99 years old, and Ishmael is his teenage son. Here we see that Sarah's character still needs some work. Now succumbing to her situation (she's decades past mothering age, and jaded beyond belief), Sarah laughs at the Lord's promise when it comes again (Genesis 20:12). It appears at this point she had more doubt than faith. The wrinkles, the weak limbs, the deflated ego, and the defeated life circumstances—Sarah couldn't even dream anymore, she had been waiting so long. She laughed, not a hopeful laugh, but a baffled one; a baby next year? Is it even worth entertaining the thought? Sarah had given up, and when her lack of faith is called into question, she lies, out of fear of being truly known by God (Genesis 18:15).

It appears this fear of the Lord is Sarah's saving grace. After God exposed her doubt, she seemingly accepted that He truly was in control. The writer of Hebrews says that it was by faith that Sarah was able to have her child and as a result, she judges God faithful (Hebrews 11:11).

In the end, God keeps His Word, and eventually gives Sarah her promised child, Isaac (Genesis 21:1), and it happens exactly at the time God said it would. Sarah does the right thing in praising God for His faithfulness (Genesis 21:6), but she still doesn't change her selfish and controlling ways. Just as quickly, another fight between the women erupts, as Sarah remembers that Ishmael might still have a right to Abraham's inheritance. She takes this opportunity to demand Hagar and her son be sent away. What ensues is a heartbreaking departure, both for Abraham, who has to send his firstborn son and second wife into the wilderness (Genesis 21:11), and for Hagar, who has no idea what will happen to them there. In both instances God meets them where they are, providing comfort and assurance that He is still in control. He visits Hagar when all hope is lost, when resources have run out and she sees nothing ahead but death (Genesis 21:16). It's in that moment when her heart cries that God draws near, with His way of making a path in the wilderness. In fact, He makes a whole new life for her in the wilderness. Ishmael grows up to be a strong and skilled archer (Genesis 21:20-21), and he and Hagar live a long and fruitful life.

Abraham and Sarah enjoy their son Isaac, and we know he also grows up to be a blessed and favored man of God. But it's also worth noting that, in a time when God allowed people to live hundreds of years, Sarah died at age 127 (Genesis 23:2). She doesn't live to see Isaac get married to Rebecca. And her husband Abraham mourns, but eventually marries a woman named Keturah. Could it be that Sarah cut her own life short with antics of jealousy, anger, control, and defiance?

This is a cautionary tale about being the cause of your own problems. Sarah is an example of what not to do with a promise from God. We see in Abraham what Sarah's faith should look like. We see in Hagar what Sarah's obedience to God should look like. We see a grace from God that is beyond what she deserved; after all, He could have condemned her. He could have scolded her. He could have decided not to give her a baby simply because of her behavior, and it would have made sense to the rest of us. But He didn't. Instead, God gives her joy in the midst of her own contrived chaos. He redeems her lost years. He silences her critics. And He blesses her so that we can see how merciful, gracious, and faithful He is.

THE WOMANHOOD OF SARAH AND HAGAR

Sarah is devoted to her husband Abraham and her family. She listens for Abraham's direction when they go to the Egyptian Pharaoh (Genesis 12:12), contrives a plan for her servant to bear a child when she can't (Genesis 16), and later she defends her son Isaac when she perceives he's being mocked by Ishmael (Genesis 21:9). All of these instances reflect a heart of loyalty and commitment. We see her determination in achieving a goal, doing whatever it takes to make it happen. This is an admirable quality when done correctly, and most importantly, when done with God's direction.

Sarah also has traits we as women should take care not to emulate. Most obviously, she takes matters into her own hands in moments of impatience while waiting for God to fulfill His promises. We see bitterness, jealousy, and manipulation in her dealings with Hagar, and a worldly desire to be perceived a certain way, which she prioritizes above truly serving God in her household. And while God is gracious and gives her joy in Isaac's birth, we see Sarah return to fighting with Hagar over her position in the house, which is essentially a result of her pride.

On the other hand, Hagar demonstrates humility and obedience in a situation in which she could have been defiant and unwilling to submit. She not only served her mistress faithfully before being told to have Abraham's child, but she also remained loyal even when the plan fell apart and she was scorned. Hagar grows into her confidence and authority when she becomes a mother, which challenges Sarah, but also reflects her own newly developed pride. Later we see that Hagar submits to God's direction to endure, even in her unfavorable environment. She leans on Him too, especially in her single motherhood, which inspires God to provide, protect, and ultimately, bless her and her son.

Take a moment to reflect on Sarah and Hagar's womanhood:

What similarities do you see to your own?

What character flaws do they each demonstrate, and what are their redemptive qualities?

Write down your biggest takeaway about God from Sarah and Hagar's story below:

RACHEL & LEAH

Read: Genesis 29-31

How do we see God while facing rejection from men?

Centuries ago, the plural relationship dynamic was not seen as a spectacle; many cultures and societies considered polygamy normal, or even aspirational. From Abraham and Jacob (who we'll talk about here with Rachel and Leah), all the way to David and Solomon—men having multiple wives was commonly shown throughout the Bible. But it's important to note that it isn't ever shown to be a good thing in the Bible. Since polygamy goes against God's original design for a union between one man and one woman, this perversion of marriage yields what any other perversion of God's plan typically yields: an environment of conflict, brokenness, and destruction.

One of the most famous examples of polygamy in the Bible is the original "sister wives" duo, Rachel and Leah, both married to Jacob. Their story, which we read in Genesis 29, presents several themes important to godly womanhood, including beauty, value, and expectations in marriage; the outcome of manipulation and control; and once again, the concept of divine purpose.

Jacob finds himself in Paddam Aran at the doorstep of his uncle Laban after running away at his mother Rebecca's instruction to avoid the anger of his brother Esau (Genesis 29:1). There, Jacob first meets Rachel, who was technically his cousin, and becomes enamored with her. Rachel's older sister Leah is introduced as having "weak eyes" in comparison to her younger, beautiful sister who is described as having a "lovely figure" (Genesis 29:17). While it's unclear what "weak eyes" means—either Leah had a noticeable vision impairment, or this was a polite way of saying she was not attractive—the Bible postulates the two women in contrast, with Rachel clearly being the more desirable choice.

In exchange for working for Laban for seven years, Jacob seeks Rachel's hand in marriage but is tricked into marrying Leah first by their father. We can already see an environment of dysfunction and deceit in Laban's household (which includes Rebecca—she and Jacob were guilty of deception too). Not only did Laban trick his nephew with a dishonest contract of labor, he also arranged the marriage deal without regard for either of his daughters' feelings about being sold off. Rachel expected she would be marrying the man she'd fallen in love with alone and now had to share, while Leah was callously inserted into the situation, only to be met with rejection at every turn.

Nonetheless, Jacob agrees, the wedding takes place, and the groom goes to consummate his marriage with the wife he worked hard to acquire. The Bible doesn't explain how Jacob didn't know it wasn't Rachel he slept with that night (Genesis 29:25), but some Jewish traditions posit that Rachel remained silent out of compassion for her unwed sister, sacrificing her love so Leah could get married first (Kadari, 2009). After Jacob realizes the deception and finds himself married to Leah, Laban attempts to explain their custom of marrying the oldest daughter first, leading to Jacob agreeing to work another seven years to get Rachel as well. The act of using Leah as a bargaining tool in the marriage arrangement says a lot about how she was viewed and valued by her father, by Jacob, and even by the culture of the day. Because of her appearance being described as less desirable than Rachel, and her singleness as the older sister, we can assume that Laban was concerned about the optics of his older daughter being unwed. Leah also has to contend with Jacob's willingness to go through with the marriage only to get her sister Rachel (Genesis 29:30). The rejection from her father, now reinforced by her husband, must have been damaging to her self-esteem and understanding of her worth.

We get the first glimpse of hope for Leah in the confirmation that God saw that she was unloved (Genesis 29:31). He saw all of the rejection from the men in her life, and stepped in as her Heavenly Father to show that she was indeed loved by Him. God gives Leah children, while Rachel remains childless. But Leah's flawed humanity also begins to show once her children become a part of the story. Instead of thanking God for His blessings and the gift of motherhood, Leah is focused on gaining Jacob's affection with this apparent advantage she now has over her sister Rachel. She names her first son Reuben, saying "The Lord has noticed my misery, and now my husband will love me" (Genesis 29:32). Leah expected that having children would give her the upper hand in the relationship and finally make Jacob love her. After all, their society esteemed women who bore children, especially sons, and ostracized women who were barren like Rachel.

Despite not seeing the love she desired from Jacob come to fruition after having her first son, Leah's fixation on winning Jacob's heart continues with the births of two more of her children. With Simeon, she declares "The Lord heard that I was unloved and has given me another son" (Genesis 29:33). And when her third son Levi was born, Leah's first thought was "surely this time my husband will feel affection for me, since I have given him three sons!" (Genesis 29:34). It isn't until she gives birth to Judah, her fourth son, that Leah's focus shifts back to God. Perhaps it became clear to her that Jacob was not changing his mind, so with Judah's birth Leah declares, "Now I will praise the Lord!" (Genesis 29:35). It's interesting that women today sometimes make a similar mistake, thinking that they can gain a man's affection or attention by having his children. The consequence of Eve's sin rings true in Leah's situation—she desired to control her husband, but he ruled over her (Genesis 3:16). His love was never a guarantee, despite her attempts.

Leah's apparent obsession with her circumstances demonstrates a humanness, and a womanhood, that is also very familiar. When women seek the validation of men, it pulls us away from the acceptance and love of God. When women hold on to our idea of a perfect outcome, we diminish the work of God in our lives and His ability to do exceedingly, abundantly beyond what we could think of, ask or imagine (Ephesians 3:20). Leah's desire for Jacob's attention and her craving for a love that was never hers was little more than a foolish attempt at control. Finally, with her son Judah, Leah seemed to understand that God's love was enough. Perhaps she rested knowing that she had been blessed by God, with His favor upon her life and a calling to give birth to sons and raise a nation. Or, perhaps she just saw how frustrated Rachel had become in her barrenness and finally felt vindicated. Whatever it was, Leah finally rests in God's perfect plan.

On the other hand, Rachel began to turn on her husband, showing her true self as a woman without much faith and revealing a manipulative personality. She demanded that Jacob must give her children, or else she would die (Genesis 30:1), to which he reminds her that God is the one in control. Rachel also uses Jacob's love for her as leverage with Leah; she bargains time with him for mandrakes from Leah's son Reuben (Genesis 30:14-15). Her callous proposal suggests she knew Leah's heart desires and didn't hesitate to use them against her to get what she wanted. Later, when Jacob finally decides to leave Laban and move his family back to Canaan, Rachel stole her father's household idols (Genesis 31:19), signifying that she still trusted in the false gods, or at least believed in them, despite knowing God. Rachel also lied about being on her menstrual cycle to avoid getting up to reveal she had taken the idols. We women have been using our periods as an excuse since ancient times.

In truth, Rachel and Leah's feud was fueled by control, manipulation, societal pressure, and jealousy rather than a true desire to have children. They disregard both Jacob and the children at one point, instead looking to prove their womanhood and exert power over each other. Similar to her husband's grandmother Sarah, Rachel takes matters into her own hands and makes her servant Bilhah sleep with Jacob (Genesis 30:4-7). When Leah does the same with her servant Zilpah, what ensues is a fight of fertility between the sisters with their servant women as proxies, resulting in four more sons being born—Dan, Naphtali, Gad, and Asher (Genesis 30:6-12). Both women thought of their surrogacies with the servants as God's divine intervention, but their arrangements were orchestrated without His consultation, just like Sarah and Hagar. They begin to use Jacob as a pawn in their game against each other, sleeping with him to have more children and gain the upper hand (Genesis 30:16). Rachel and Leah also saw Jacob as a means of escape from their father Laban (Genesis 31:15). They quickly realized that Laban's deceit had robbed them both of the futures they imagined for themselves, and they willingly left home to pursue the inheritance God had given Jacob.

In the end, Rachel died giving birth to her last son Benjamin (Genesis 35:16-18), which begs the question: was it all worth it? While the competition between Rachel and Leah still produced the sons that would later become the twelve tribes of Israel, their relationships with each other, their husband, and their father remained dysfunctional until Rachel's death.

Despite Rachel and Leah's interferences, God's plan to establish the nation of Israel prevails, and in the end Leah is honored for her faith. Her sons play a significant role in the formation of the tribes of Israel, with Levi's descendants becoming the priestly tribe and Judah establishing the lineage of King David, which ultimately leads to Jesus. And despite his initial love for Rachel, in the end, Jacob is buried next to Leah (Genesis 49:29). The Bible implies that the wife whose faithfulness to God and whose wisdom and virtue illuminated her inner beauty prevailed in the end over the one whose physical beauty hid an underlying weakness of character.

God still remembered Rachel (Genesis 30:22). He allowed her to birth Joseph and Benjamin, whose lineages proved to be significant in the history of Israel and the orchestration of God's plan of redemption. Joseph is well known for his story of being sold into slavery by his jealous brothers, rising to the position of Vizier in Egypt, and ultimately saving the nation and his own family from famine by his interpretation of divine dreams (Genesis 37-50). And Benjamin's family line leads to King Saul and the apostle Paul. Rachel's story is a testament to the faithfulness of God, whose ultimate plan of redemption gives us grace to make these mistakes and still be called worthy. Despite her flaws, and our flaws, God remains merciful and faithful.

THE WOMANHOOD OF RACHEL AND LEAH

The story of Rachel and Leah is an example of how God can use imperfect individuals and families to fulfill His purposes, despite their flaws and sinful behaviors. Through these women's lives we see God's sovereignty and fairness as He rewards and punishes. We can also take the lesson from Leah's life that our true worth comes from God when we allow Him to fulfill His will in our lives, not from earthly desires and validation from men. God blessed Leah with children knowing she was the less-favored wife; Rachel, though loved by her husband, is humbled by the Lord. The characters of both women are shown throughout the story: Leah eventually displays faith and trust in the will of God, while Rachel's lack of faith and manipulative tactics reveal her weakness of character. In the end, God hears both of their prayers, reflecting His mercy towards us even when we don't deserve it.

Take a moment to reflect on Rachel and Leah's womanhood:

What similarities do you see to your own?

What character flaws do they each demonstrate, and what are their redemptive qualities?

Write down your biggest takeaway about God from Rachel and Leah's story below:

RAHAB

Read: Joshua 2

Would you give up your home, your community, and your culture for God?

Prostitution is one of the oldest professions in the world. Money in exchange for sex; fantasies fulfilled with strangers; late nights and street corners; hidden rooms and hushed secrets. Society looks down on women who decide to pursue this career, but rarely condemns the men who seek after them. On the subject of prostitution, the Church focuses on how deplorable a life of sex work is and how a woman who decides to live that life is loose and lost. After all, a woman having sex for money tells you everything you need to know about her, right? Rarely do we stop to consider the thought that maybe, just maybe, there is more to a prostitute than what she does for a living.

Now, Rahab's story, and its inclusion in the Bible (and this book), is in no way an endorsement of prostitution as a godly lifestyle or career choice for a woman of Christian values. Rahab was not a Christian; she wasn't even an Israelite. But it is clear that Rahab's life was one that God used for His purposes, to achieve His plan of redemption for Israel. There is certainly something special about this woman. Not only is Rahab the only person named in Joshua 2 (we don't even learn the name of the king or the spies), her brief story interrupts the ongoing saga of Israel's conquest of the Promised Land throughout the book of Joshua. We later learn that Rahab is noted as one of the women who God placed in the royal family of David and the divine lineage of Jesus Christ (Matthew 1:5). Here in the book of Joshua we learn why—it's her faith.

The Bible doesn't give us much information about Rahab's background, but she is noted as the owner of a house on Jericho's wall (Joshua 2:15). Jericho was believed to be a Canaanite military station (Eames, 2024). Travelers stopping at Rahab's house may have been looking for a good night's sleep on their long routes, perhaps a meal or drink, and yes, also sex. Her house was built into the city wall, which was soon to be doomed to destruction with the rest of Jericho because of the Canaanites' idol worship (Deuteronomy 12:2-3). The city was full of wickedness in the eyes of God. It was filled with people who worshipped a variety of false gods, including Baal and Asherah, gods and goddesses that glorified sex, fertility, and war, and whose rituals involved prostitution and child sacrifice.

Throughout the Bible, prostitution figuratively illustrates the concept of idolatry. Idols are anything—whether objects, people, or concepts—that take the place of God in our lives. So, prostitution is used to illustrate what happens when we operate on our own accord outside of a relationship with God. Prostitution represents how far away the desires of the flesh can pull us from our God-given purpose and into something destructive. Men are told to stay away from the prostitute; women are told to avoid becoming one. Followers of God are told that idol worship is essentially the same thing. But with Rahab, we have an example of a prostitute who chooses God.

Rahab's world is changed by the series of fateful events that see Joshua, the newly-appointed leader of the Israelite army, sending out two spies to survey the doomed city of Jericho ahead of its takedown (Joshua 2:1-2). The spies make their way to her house, and she decides to hide them from the king's soldiers. When word gets to the king of Jericho that the prostitute is harboring spies, he sends men to her house to capture them. Rahab lies, telling the king's men that the spies enjoyed her services only for a short time and that they had already made their way out of town (Joshua 2:2-4). She leads the soldiers away from her house, and as soon as they leave, Rahab returns to her hidden visitors to make a poignant request: *when you take down this city, spare me and my family* (Joshua 2:12). The spies agree with caution. In exchange, they tell Rahab to signify her allegiance to them and God by hanging a scarlet rope in her window, and they instruct her to keep all of her relatives inside when they return (Joshua 2:18). Immediately, Rahab agrees.

It's important to remember that Rahab wasn't a believer. She may have seen an opportunity to escape pending doom by siding with the Israelite spies, but what convinced her that they would be successful in their takeover of Jericho? Rahab told the men she heard about the God of Israel (Joshua 2:10) and that everyone in town was afraid, including her. This wasn't just an opportunity to flee from danger; Rahab's capacity for faith becomes evident when she declares that she knows the God of the Israelite spies is *the one true God* (Joshua 2:11).

We have to look closer at Rahab's character to understand how she could get to the point of acting in faith, and how she could actually represent the heart of God without even knowing Him. In her we see a wise and discerning woman of conviction, although employed in a profession that most people today consider shameful. Jericho was an enclosure of Canaanite hedonism and depravity, with its people primarily focused on the wealth they enjoyed, the gods they worshiped, and the morally corrupt rituals and practices that ensued (Mackie & Sullivan, 2017). Perhaps Rahab longed for something different than the culture she knew in Jericho. Her promised land may have looked like freedom from a depraved society. Perhaps she wanted a new life, a fresh start, and ultimately the protection that the God of Israel was offering to those who believed in Him. Rahab was ready and willing to walk away from a life of vulnerability and insecurity in Jericho for something more—a life of peace and fulfillment with God.

Rahab was a selfless woman. She had brothers and sisters, parents and extended family; without hesitation, in her agreement with the spies, Rahab decided to save them too (Joshua 2:12-13). Imagine the courage it takes to forsake everything you've known, the life and home you've built, and the friends and community you've loved. Then, imagine the conviction it takes to bring your family along. They may not have agreed with the plan; they may have wanted to stay in Jericho, but Rahab resolved that she could not let them perish. Here she stepped into boldness as an evangelist, poised to tell her unbelieving family about God.

Rahab's open and willing heart of faith is what God saw fit to honor and highlight for generations to come. By sending the spies to her house, He provided an opportunity, or perhaps even a test, for Rahab to profess out loud what she truly believed in her heart (Joshua 2:11). The spies responded to what God was doing in her life, and they were obedient and faithful to see it through. They agreed to save a pagan woman and her family, but in exchange they asked her to make a public declaration of her newfound faith represented by the display of the scarlet rope. Many scholars have determined the rope to be a foreshadowing of the blood of Jesus and a parallel to the Passover Lamb, both representing the covenant of safety through which those who believe in God are ensured everlasting protection (Bonesteele, 2022).

Finally, Rahab's status as a prostitute tells us something about the character of God. Even when dealing with sinful people, even in the context of a morally corrupt society, God is still ready to receive those who are brave enough to put their faith and trust in Him. It's a beautiful reminder of the gospel message—that while we were still sinners, Christ died for us (Romans 5:6-8).

In Rahab's story, God looks lovingly at His rebellious child, ignoring the prostitute label everyone has placed on her to give her a new name: worthy daughter. Her story is for the woman who longs for something new; the one who has felt empty and numb from an unfulfilled life of sin, with a void in her heart that no man has been able to fill and a reputation that puts her on the outskirts of society. He is offering her a scarlet rope to freedom.

God erased the wounds and ways of Rahab's past and wrote a new story, giving her a new life direction that changed the course of her future and all of history at the same time. He tenderly dressed the wounds of her heart and created in her a clean slate, setting a foundation from which she would learn how to worship. That's the God that Rahab chose to align with, and He is still worthy of losing everything just to find Him.

THE WOMANHOOD OF RAHAB

Rahab represents a level of faith and conviction that is celebrated to this day. While she wasn't an Israelite, she saw an opportunity to align herself with the One True God in a bold declaration of faith that defies her king, her pagan culture, and the gods she may have previously served. Her actions reflect that faith without works is dead (James 2:17). Not only did she claim to believe in God, she was also obedient to the spies' instructions. With the scarlet rope, she saved herself and her family. We are reminded of Rahab's declaration of faith in the book of Hebrews, where she is commemorated for trusting God (Hebrews 11:31). For Rahab, seeing wasn't necessary for believing. The evidence was present; even hearing of His mighty works was enough for her to declare that He alone was God. For her, to believe in God was to know of His power and might to redeem and restore—and actually want to see it at work.

Take a moment to reflect on Rahab's womanhood:

What similarities do you see to your own?

What character flaws does she demonstrate, and what are her redemptive qualities?

Write down your biggest takeaway about God from Rahab's story below:

RUTH & NAOMI

Read: Ruth 1-4

What does loyalty to the women in your life look like?

In today's popular culture, it's rare to find an example of a healthy, happy relationship between a mother and daughter-in-law. Or any intergenerational relationship between women, for that matter. When it comes to family dynamics, mainstream media always seems to put mothers and daughters-in-law against each other, rather than showing a loving relationship between women of different generations. We know that popular culture tends to devalue a woman as she gets older, and we've seen plenty of examples of this "monster-in-law" dynamic; in fact there is a famous movie with the same name. "Monster-in-law" usually means the older woman is overbearing, controlling, cold, or even cruel to her son's wife, while the young woman does everything she can to keep her in-law out of their lives. The coldness and callousness women of different generations have toward each other represents our deep-rooted competition to gain value in the eyes of society.

Let's pause for a moment and wonder why these relationships are portrayed in such a negative light. Of course, it's the work of the enemy to distort and divide women across generations when the Bible advocates for unity. God, through the words of the apostle Paul, instructs older women to teach the younger ones (Titus 2:3-5). The reason is that biblical sisterhood is powerful and divine. When done correctly, as with the stories of women like Ruth and her mother-in-law Naomi, or others like Mary and Elizabeth or even the daughters of Zelophehad, true biblical sisterhood unites women in the eternal pursuit of Christ, for His glory to be seen through our womanhood, and His character to be reflected by our devotion to each other (Baker, 2020). Perhaps there is no greater example of this type of sisterhood, love, and loyalty than the story of Ruth and Naomi.

One of the most common teachings from the book of Ruth centers around how she finds a suitable husband in Boaz after the tragedy of losing her husband Mahlon. We emphasize the type of man Boaz represents, and we declare that he is what women should be looking for in a man today. The Church tends to highlight Ruth for her meekness, loyalty, and kindness to Naomi, but tends to suggest the outcome of her doing so was the divine favor she received to remarry. More importantly, Ruth's story is about the redemptive love of God and the incredible faith and trust that this Moabite woman, a pagan and foreigner, puts in the God of Israel. She is also a worthy example of humility and submission. It is Ruth's loyalty to God, her mother-in-law, Boaz, and her new Israelite family that speaks to her character and highlights God's redemptive work in her life.

Ruth's story begins with a famine in Israel (Ruth 1:1), which leads Naomi's husband Elimelek to move his family to Moab. There, his two sons, Mahlon and Kilion, married Moabite women named Ruth and Orpah, but then all of the men died, leaving Naomi and her two daughters-in-law as widows (Ruth 1:4-5). Naomi, Ruth, and Orpah found solace and comfort in each other after their tragic losses. The two younger women were kind to their mother-in-law (Ruth 1:8), and in turn Naomi called them her daughters, imparting her wisdom and teaching them in the ways of the Lord. When Naomi decided to move back to Judah, she told Ruth and Orpah to stay in Moab and find new lives, but they both refused (Ruth 1:10). She explained to the women that fulfilling the Jewish custom of marrying within the family after their husbands died would not be possible; Naomi was too old to remarry and have more sons (Ruth 1:11-13). Instead, she released Ruth and Orpah from their obligation, telling them to start new lives in Moab. But Ruth still refused. She beautifully stated, "Where you go I will go, and where you stay I will stay. Your people will be my people and your God my God" (Ruth 1:16).

Ruth's declaration of faith and loyalty is admirable, but so is Naomi's quiet faith throughout what was likely the lowest moments of her life. Elimelek moved his family from God's land in Judah to Moab at a time of famine. Doing so suggested Elimelek may have been fearful; he chose to relocate his family to a pagan society instead of remaining in the Promised Land and trusting in God to protect his family there. Then, while in Moab he and his sons died, and Naomi was left alone (Ruth 1:5), but she maintained her faith in God. When the famine was over, she decided to go back to Judah, back under the Lord's protection. While we don't know why God allowed her husband and sons to die (could it be because they abandoned their faith?), Naomi shared her heart with her daughters-in-law, saying that the Lord had raised His fist against her (Ruth 1:13). Her faith had taken a hit after such heartbreaking losses, and it's understandable that she found it hard to see a positive future for herself. But Ruth's profound words of loyalty served as the injection of faith that Naomi needed. The Lord showed her that she was not alone.

In Hebrew, Ruth's name means "friend" or "companion," which is fitting as it describes the role she played for her mother-in-law Naomi and later her husband Boaz. As a Moabite, Ruth would have been raised to believe in false gods, but she chose to marry and accept the beliefs of her Israelite husband Mahlon and his family, and she submitted to learning from Naomi. When Ruth was given the opportunity to return home and start a new life, she refused, showing immense loyalty, courage, and kindness to Naomi by pledging to die with her (Ruth 1:17). By declaring "your people will be my people, and your God my God," not only did Ruth choose to stay with Naomi, but she also chose the God of Israel—forsaking any others. From her decision onward, we see God begin to write her new life story, under His protection, in Judah.

Naomi was apparently still struggling with faith when they arrived in Bethlehem. She openly expressed her sorrow, telling people that she wouldn't answer to her name, which meant "pleasantness," "delight," and "beauty" in Hebrew. Instead, she wanted to be called Mara, which meant "bitter," reflecting her heart posture (Ruth 1:20). We have to be careful not to hold bitterness towards the Lord when we face hardship. The Bible says to consider it an opportunity for great joy when troubles come our way, for when faith is tested, endurance has a chance to grow (James 1:2-4). Naomi's faith had been tested, and it wouldn't be long before the Lord would begin to change her story.

By God's divine providence, Ruth began harvesting in the fields of Naomi's relative Boaz, who soon noticed her work ethic and heard about her loyalty to Naomi (Ruth 2:5-6). Boaz offered his protection to Ruth while she worked, impressed by her devotion and selflessness. He created a safe environment for her to harvest, ensuring she would be taken care of by his servants and treated well (Ruth 2:5-11). Boaz offering safety and security is not a coincidence. Naomi revealed to Ruth that Boaz was actually her family's guardian-redeemer (Ruth 2:20), a legal term in Jewish society which made him responsible for a relative's well-being in times of trouble (Robinson, 1993). Both literally and symbolically, Boaz becomes the guardian and redeemer for Ruth. Moved by her actions, his first response was to protect and provide for her; then later, he moved to reward her selflessness and loyalty by restoring her honor in marriage. His actions reflect the character of God as our protector, provider and redeemer.

Upon hearing the news, Naomi's faith becomes evident again—she has hope for Ruth and Boaz. She returns the kindness and loyalty she received from Ruth by devising a plan to secure a future for the young widow with her relative (Ruth 3:1). Ruth submitted to Naomi's plan with humility, vowing to do exactly as she was told (Ruth 3:5). She made herself available to Boaz with a vulnerable but significant gesture, laying at his feet, which indicated she wanted to become his wife (Smith, 2026). Ruth's humble heart stood out to Boaz, who was a much older man. He acknowledged that she could have taken interest in a much younger or richer man (Ruth 3:10). Ruth's actions showed her level of trust in God and her willingness to submit to His plan.

After approving Boaz's request to marry Ruth, the witnesses and elders bestow upon her several important blessings of legacy and esteem in Israel (Ruth 4:11). They declare that Boaz's new wife would be like Rachel and Leah, whose sons become the nation of Israel. They also compare Ruth to Tamar, praying she would birth a son like Perez who represents God's divine purpose bursting forth (Ruth 11:12). God directly answers this prayer, honoring Ruth's faithfulness by placing her in the lineage of royalty as the great-grandmother of King David, and ultimately in the family and ancestry of Jesus Christ (Ruth 4:18-22). By marrying Boaz, Ruth also inherited a new mother-in-law, who happened to be Rahab (Matthew 1:5). By God's divine orchestration, He gives Boaz a wife whose admirable faith resembles that of his mother.

As for Naomi, her joy was restored when Ruth gave birth to Obed, and she cared for the baby as if he were her own (Ruth 4:16). The women of the town made an important declaration as they gave praise to God for the son of Naomi's daughter-in-law, who they say had been better to her than seven sons (Ruth 4:15). God chose Ruth to be the vessel through which He would display his immense love for Naomi. Their divine sisterhood would be the avenue through which He would restore her family name, and ultimately, God also used Ruth to restore Naomi's faith in Him.

THE WOMANHOOD OF RUTH & NAOMI

Ruth is celebrated for her unshakable loyalty to Naomi, her courage and obedience in the midst of an uncertain future, and her willingness to commit to the one true God. Ruth also displays loyalty and humble submission to both Naomi and Boaz. What makes Ruth special isn't necessarily her appearance. She isn't lauded for her beauty, strength or courage—although these are all qualities that she certainly possessed. It's clear that her reputation of selflessness and loyalty left a lasting impression on everyone who heard her story, including Boaz. Ruth is unique in that her beauty radiated from her heart. From her faith and loyalty, the strength of her character shined for all to see. Ruth's life story is a reflection of love and loyalty to God, and her redemption and protection by Boaz represents the same given to us through Jesus Christ, our own guardian-redeemer. In Ruth we also see an example of the kind of helpmate that God intends for a woman to be for everyone around her—not just to a man.

Naomi displays a godly nurturing quality as a mother-in-law to Ruth and Orpah. Instead of mistreating or looking down on the foreign wives her sons married, she guides them in the ways of the Lord, and provides comfort and care when they all tragically lose their husbands. Although the difficult circumstances took a toll on Naomi's faith, she returned to Judah with Ruth by her side and trusted in the Lord to carry out his perfect plan of redemption for her family through Boaz. Her joy is restored with Ruth and Boaz's marriage and the birth of their son Obed, and Naomi leads the women of the town in giving all praises to God.

Take a moment to reflect on Ruth and Naomi's womanhood:

What similarities do you see to your own?

What character flaws do they demonstrate, and what are their redemptive qualities?

Write down your biggest takeaway about God from Ruth and Naomi's story below:

ESTHER

Read: Esther 1-10

What does it mean to be made queen for such a time as this?

In popular culture Queen Esther and the book of Esther have been represented as a rags-to-riches, almost fairytale story of a beautiful girl who saved a nation by winning the heart of a king. The story typically centers a narrative about Esther's beauty and courage, and the king's attraction to her, without giving much attention to Esther's character and her admirable attributes like faith, humility, and submission to God and to the men in positions of authority around her. From humble beginnings as an orphan raised by her older cousin Mordecai to her outstanding faith and relationship with God, Esther's story has much more depth and wisdom about biblical womanhood than popular culture lets on.

Esther is one of only two women who make up an entire book of the Bible, the other being Ruth. And in both books, the women exemplify humility, kindness, and commitment to God and the Jewish people. While Ruth is a foreigner brought into the Israelite community through her loyalty to her husband's family, Esther rose to a position of prominence as the new queen of a foreign land, Persia, enabling her to preserve her Jewish people and heritage. Ultimately, God used both women to ensure the continuation of His plan and people.

The teenage Esther and her older cousin Mordecai were among the exiled Jews taken from Jerusalem into Babylon (Esther 2:6) and who later ended up in Persia, where they lived peacefully amongst the Persians under King Xerxes. When his wife Vashti defied him, the king was advised to establish a harem of young and beautiful virgins, eventually choosing one to replace her. Esther was taken among them (Esther 2:8). She was then forced into competition with hundreds of other beautiful women, where she is essentially trained to become the concubine of a petulant king whose impulsive behavior could mean life or death.

It's in this dire situation that we get the first admirable example of Esther's character: her obedience and submission. From the moment she entered Xerxes's haram, Esther was destined only to please him for the rest of her life. Despite the tragedy of her situation, Esther doesn't sit and sulk in her circumstances. Instead, she does what she is told by the eunuch Hegai, keeping in mind everything she has been taught by her cousin Mordecai, who is divinely put in a position to stay close to her and guide her through her time in the palace (Esther 2:11). Esther allows Hegai to tell her what to do, what to wear, and ultimately how to prepare herself to be the best choice for the king (Esther 2:9). In the harem, Esther and the other women had to wait for the king to summon them; after a night with him they would leave, unsure of when their next encounter would take place. There was always a chance that the king would never ask for them again. Esther was ready when her time came, and she did only what Hegai told her (Esther 2:16). As a result of her humility and obedience, Esther was favored by the king, Hegai, and everyone else she encountered.

Throughout the story, and despite becoming queen, Esther still also fully submitted herself to the guidance of Mordecai, who raised her like his own daughter.

One can only imagine the haram environment. It was probably similar to a beauty pageant dressing room, with Esther surrounded by scores of other beautiful women who envisioned themselves as queen. She likely faced jealousy from the others as she emerged the clear favorite for Hegai and the other eunuchs. Her days may have been filled with their cattiness, pettiness, rumors, and hatred. The other women probably thought, *what exactly makes Esther the best?* Perhaps they even plotted against her. In the end, the king loved Esther the most, leading to her elevation to queen (Esther 2:17).

Now, for a moment we have to talk about Queen Vashti, whom Esther replaced. Your inclination might be to defend Vashti for her refusal to be paraded before the king's drunken guests solely for her beauty as another display of his wealth (Esther 1:10-12). Surely as women we can understand why she refused. Some Bible scholars believe that King Xerxes was actually asking Vashti to come out naked, only wearing the royal crown (*Got Questions Ministries*, 2022). The king did not take her feelings or comfort about doing so into consideration, nor did he care that his wife was in the middle of throwing her own banquet for the noble women. For her defiance, and in his anger, the King consulted his advisors to seek a punishment for her refusal of the order. Not only did she say no to the king, she had done so in a public and embarrassing way. The noble men made the case that many of their wives and other women of the kingdom would become equally defiant, empowered by Vashti's action. They convinced the king that he had to make an example of Vashti in order to stop them from losing control of their wives, essentially stopping the women from igniting a feminist movement (Esther 1:17-18).

As justifiable as her actions were, there is a mistake that Vashti makes here which serves as a lesson for godly women to learn. If through the story of Esther we learn how wisdom and submission to God and authority work in our favor, then through the story of Vashti we see an example of what happens when we don't submit. The issue is less about appeasing a drunk king in his revelry and more about walking in humility. In essence, Vashti's mistake can be described as biting the hand that feeds you. In today's society, Queen Vashti would have been celebrated for taking a stand against the patriarchy. But in those days it was an act of defiance. Vashti was queen, and she enjoyed the luxuries and comforts involved in being queen for years. And in this moment, perhaps she didn't count the cost of her actions. As a result of her mutiny, not only does Vashti lose her status as queen, but every woman in the kingdom is forced by law to submit to their husbands (Esther 1:22).

Although it was God's plan for Vashti to be dethroned and for Esther to become queen, the lesson from Vashti's actions for us as women is that true submission requires wisdom and restraint. Whether with family, in one's workplace, at church, or even with God, it isn't wise to dishonor authority and expect a good outcome. In fact, it's foolish. After living with this king for years and knowing his personality, Queen Vashti, of all people, should have known how Xerxes would react to her refusal. Perhaps she could have asked to speak with the king in private or even presented a better idea, suggesting another method to display his wealth that didn't involve her to appease his boastful desires. Vashti represents a sort of defiance that isn't godly. In contrast, Esther does not challenge authority, but instead trusts God and the counsel around her to ensure she will be taken care of in her submission.

It's also important that we acknowledge Queen Vashti's beauty and look at it in contrast to Esther's. It's easy to forget that Vashti was also known to be the most beautiful woman in the land and the prized possession of the king for this reason; he took every opportunity to show her off (Esther 1:11). If Queen Vashti was dethroned because of something other than her beauty, then it makes sense that Esther was made queen because of something other than her beauty. Xerxes was enamored with Esther, and not just in the physical way that he was with Vashti. He didn't parade Esther's beauty in a show of authority; instead, he submitted to it and gave her the authority. After sleeping with her (Esther 2:17), even with all of the other virgins he had to choose from, Xerxes eventually came to the point where he wanted to please *her* over himself (Esther 5:3).

Aside from Esther's beauty and humility, there's a lot we can take away about her faith. From the moment she entered the palace, Esther concealed her Jewish identity at Mordecai's instruction (Esther 2:10). He was well aware that doing so would protect her from any prejudice from palace officials. While Jewish people lived among the Persians, they were still regarded as second-class citizens. Mordecai likely wanted to ensure that Esther's chances of being chosen as queen would not be affected by anyone's perceptions of her people, and for good reason, as we see Haman's disdain of the Jewish people play a significant role in what happens next (Esther 3:6). He explains to the king that the Jews are different, keeping themselves separate from the Persians and practicing different customs (Esther 3:8). What he really meant was that the Jews were obedient to their God above all else; they would never bow down to men like Haman.

When the Jews were sentenced to death with Haman's decree (Esther 3:13), Esther had to take action on behalf of her people. Mordecai explained to her that she was put in position for a moment like this (Esther 4:14), as the only Jewish person with influence over the king. But Esther was also well aware of the risk; the punishment for appearing before Xerxes out of his favor, or even speaking out of turn, was death. Moreover, she hadn't been called into the king's presence in over 30 days (Esther 4:11). Esther was probably fearful and insecure about their relationship and whether the king would kill her for speaking so boldly out of his favor. After having been ignored for so long, she likely worried that she was destined to live out the rest of her days with the other concubines in a second harem.

The strategy to combat all of those horrible possibilities was to fast and pray first. For three days, Esther, Mordecai, and all of the Jews would seek God for His divine intervention in the situation. Esther put aside her fears of what would happen, stepped out in faith, put others before herself, and resolved to suffer whatever consequences could lay ahead, stating "if I perish, I perish" (Esther 4:16). This is exactly why Esther was a worthy queen; her willingness to die for her people resembled that of Jesus Christ.

With God's divine favor the king held out his scepter and immediately pledged to grant whatever wish Esther had. But even then, she didn't make known her request to spare the Jews from being killed. Instead, her strategy was to invite the king and Haman to a banquet for two nights, allowing another three days for the Lord to intervene and work out His plan of salvation for the Jews (Esther 5:5-9). In this time, Haman plots to kill Mordecai, while God works behind the scenes to redeem and elevate Mordecai (Esther 6:1-14).

Finally, Esther's third banquet for the king and Haman takes place, and it is at this moment that God has made all things work together for the good of the Jews. Esther reveals her request that the Jews would be spared (Esther 7:3). With humility, obedience, and submission to the king, she explains that Haman's decree pronounced the death of her people. The king sees Haman for who he truly is, and conveniently, the king also learns about the pole set up at Haman's house to impale Mordecai (Esther 7:10). In the end, Esther didn't have to do too much to sway the king. He willingly gave her everything and ensured that Mordecai was taken care of as well. Only God could intervene in such a mighty way, driven by the faith, fasting, and prayers of his faithful servants.

What does it mean to be made queen for such a time as this? It means humility, obedience, and sacrifice. Despite her high position, Esther goes humbly before God first, and then humbly to the king with a plan. She prefaces her requests with, "if it pleases the king," (Esther 8:5) displaying her submission, and she made sure to honor Mordecai as she elevated to a position of power after he guided her throughout her time in the palace (Esther 9:4).

Scholars have debated the necessity of the inclusion of the book of Esther in the canonical Bible that we have today; some say it's a story to entice Jewish pride rather than reveal important characteristics of God (Ophoff, 1942). But make no mistake, Esther's story reveals a lot about God. The lack of mention of the name of God throughout the story is, in itself, a revelation. God works in providence and through people. He may not let us in on what He's doing, but the story of Esther is the perfect example of how we can rest assured that what God is doing behind the scenes will ultimately prevail.

Esther's story is for the woman who finds herself in a position of leadership or prominence that she might feel unqualified for, perhaps facing imposter syndrome or anxiety about a big task ahead. Esther reminds us that nothing is impossible with God. It's His favor that elevates an orphan to the highest position of prominence. His grace goes with her into the palace, and His grace covers her there. Her faith, prayer, and petition honors God as the wisest counsel she could seek before making important decisions. As a result, and through such divine orchestration, God uses Queen Esther to save an entire people.

THE WOMANHOOD OF ESTHER

God knew that Esther would be a star, which her name means. She is a great example of a wise and discerning woman—smart enough to assess her environment, active in her faith, and wise to seek counsel before making major decisions, both from her earthly father figure Mordecai and from her Heavenly Father. Esther is also a great example of faith with works. She takes action instead of remaining complacent or complicit in the plan to kill the Jews. After all, as queen, she hadn't revealed her Jewish identity and didn't actually have to align herself with the Jewish people. Her character reflected humility, courage, and compassion. She did not let injustice come to pass. Esther was also strategic in her thinking and patient in her execution. She exercised discretion and prudence, all characteristics worth emulating, in the midst of waiting to see God's plan come to fruition. She honored all of the men who were placed in authority before her and took Mordecai and Hegai's advice without pride or arrogance just because she was queen. Above all, Esther was faithful, prayerful, and especially submitted to God, so that when it came time for execution of His plan, she had everything she needed to succeed. Esther's story is a great example of God's favor, faithfulness, and divine providence—He causes everything to work together for the good of those who love Him (Romans 8:28).

Take a moment to reflect on Esther's womanhood:

What similarities do you see to your own?

What character flaws does she demonstrate, and what are her redemptive qualities?

Write down your biggest takeaway about God from Esther's story below:

BATHSHEBA

Read: 2 Samuel 11, 1 Kings 1, 1 Chronicles 3

How does a woman remain humble and submitted to God in the midst of heartbreak?

This is the question that often comes to my mind when I think about Bathsheba. Her story is tragic and inspiring at the same time. Similar to Esther, Bathsheba represents a level of humility, submission, and courage that is often understated while her beauty is revered. She didn't ask for King David to interfere in her marriage, for her husband to be killed, or to even become queen. But that was her destiny, and she endured. Despite the circumstances that got her to the palace, Bathsheba takes on her royal role with grace and strategy, instilling wisdom in her son Solomon as she secures the throne for his reign. God used Bathsheba to further His royal lineage and impart His divine wisdom to the world, allowing her to give birth to a son who would become known as the wisest man to have ever lived.

Bathsheba's story in the Bible begins without her consent, but her faithfulness to God is evident through the series of events that result in her becoming queen of Israel. She didn't know she was being watched by the king, but David saw her from the palace while she took her monthly ritual bath (2 Samuel 11:1). The king was supposed to be at war that day, and Bathsheba's husband Uriah was among his best soldiers. Instead, King David had abandoned his duty to lead his troops in battle when he noticed what the Bible called Bathsheba's "unusual" beauty. In those days, a Jewish woman's ritual bathing after her monthly menstrual cycle was a sign of her devotion to God and strict adherence to Mosaic law (Richardson, 2018). She was simply doing what a woman would do to return to spiritual cleanliness after her monthly period, which rendered her unclean according to Jewish tradition. But in the middle of this faith act, Bathsheba was noticed and summoned by King David (2 Samuel 11:4). Bathsheba was a married woman, but the king was the utmost authority; David took the opportunity to exert his power, knowing that the imbalance meant that she would be subject to his will, and in this case, his adulterous desires. Bathsheba had little choice; refusing the king's advances could mean death.

Bathsheba's story goes from unfortunate to tragic when the king's actions lead to her own sorrow and heartbreak. After David slept with Bathsheba and sent her home, she discovered she was pregnant (2 Samuel 11:4). Instead of righting the wrong of his sinful behavior and confessing to Uriah that he had forced Bathsheba into adultery, David tried to persuade Uriah to sleep with his wife to make it appear that he was the one who got her pregnant (2 Samuel 11:8-13). But Uriah refused to go home, instead choosing to remain in battle with the Israelite army, so David devised a plan to have Uriah killed in battle in order to keep his sin a secret and allow him to take the widowed Bathsheba as a wife (2 Samuel 11:16-17, 27).

Bathsheba was poised to become the queen consort, but she was still heartbroken at the death of her husband. The

Bible says she mourned for Uriah for a period before becoming David's wife (2 Samuel 11:26). Her love and devotion to her husband was evident even after his death. Bathsheba's anguish must have multiplied when it became clear that the Lord was angry with David for killing Uriah. God sent the prophet Nathan to rebuke the king with a curse of discord within his family. And as a direct punishment for David's adultery, the Lord said that the child he had with Bathsheba from the affair would die (2 Samuel 12:14).

Sins like adultery rarely ever affect just one person. David's actions had generational consequences for Bathsheba. Both her husband Uriah, and her father Eliam were high-ranking members of David's royal army. Her grandfather, Ahithophel, was also one of the king's wise counselors (2 Samuel 15:12, 2 Samuel 23:34). The Bible says Ahithophel later turned on the king, supporting David's son Absalom's revolt (2 Samuel 17), likely out of anger and resentment for David's actions against his granddaughter. The king's complete disregard for the men who served him, whom he knew and trusted, resulted in the destruction of those long-built relationships and several untimely deaths in Bathsheba's family.

It's hard to imagine becoming queen in the midst of so much pain. Bathsheba endured loss after loss, but still had to perform the duties of her position and stand alongside David, which she did faithfully. How did she not resent him? How did she not question God? The Bible says that David comforted his wife (2 Samuel 12:24), and she bravely endured. In His mercy, the Lord allowed the couple to have another child, whom they named Solomon. With this blessing, we see Bathsheba become a true queen mother, determined to see her son elevated to his kingship and his legacy protected.

The curse on King David's household manifested in many of his sons rising up against him, and against each other. Toward the end of his life, when David's son Adonijah made himself king and plotted to take the throne, it was Bathsheba's intervention that changed the course of Israel's history as she advocated for her son Solomon to be the rightful heir (1 Kings 1:17). Believing that Adonijah's plan of ascension to king would result in her and Solomon's imprisonment after David's death, Bathsheba moved swiftly to ensure their future would be secured while the king was still alive. She approached David on his death bed, and reminded him of his promise to make Solomon king. The plea was supported by Nathan, the same prophet who previously pronounced God's judgement over the couple. Bathsheba's plea is presented with humility, as she prostrates before the king and exalts his decision rather than challenging his authority (1 Kings 1:31). The declaration is then confirmed with a public display of David's affirmation when Solomon is presented before the people and crowned as king (1 Kings 1:33-39). After King David died and Solomon's reign was firmly established, he made a throne for his mother, and she sat at his right hand (1 Kings 2:19).

As the author of several books in the Bible, including Proverbs, Ecclesiastes, and Song of Songs, King Solomon's close relationship with his mother Bathsheba is even reflected in his writings. Many Jewish scholars believe that the passage in Proverbs 31 ascribed to King Lemuel was actually a name for Solomon himself, which makes the mother he references Bathsheba (Proverbs 31:1). The sayings of Lemuel's mother serve as explicit warnings against the personal pitfalls that can destroy future kings. She warns against drunkenness and lust after women, and advocates for the king to "speak up and judge fairly," thereby fulfilling his duty of service to his people, particularly the poor and needy (Proverbs 31:8-9). Let's assume this is Bathsheba's advice, which the author says she taught to her son. Bathsheba had spent decades in the palace, raising her son and observing the behaviors of King David and his counterparts. Her advice to her son is to remain morally upright, avoiding sins like drunkenness and advocating for justice—all characteristics that suggest devotion to God.

Bathsheba's advice about a wife of noble character also gives Solomon a concrete idea of the type of woman he should marry (Proverbs 31:10-31). This infamous description of a woman, dubbed "The Proverbs 31 Woman," is often thought of as the pinnacle of godly womanhood. The imagery Christian teachings associate with this ideal woman tends to be a feminine and gentle homemaker, but the woman described in Proverbs 31 is strong, active and enterprising. Not only does she take care of her household (Proverbs 31:15), she is busy in the marketplace with multiple business dealings (Proverbs 31:16-19), while also being a talented seamstress (Proverbs 31:24) and attentive to the poor and needy (Proverbs 31:20). This virtuous wife is wealthy and generous, wise and kind. But most importantly, she fears the Lord (Proverbs 31:30). It makes sense that Bathsheba would want such a wife for her son. Her own devotion to God was the beginning of her wisdom in the palace.

Solomon did not adhere to his mother's advice as he grew older and more worldly as king. He had hundreds of foreign wives and concubines who led him astray into idol worship; ultimately Solomon abandoned the ways of the Lord, which led to his demise and Israel's downfall (1 Kings 11:1-13). While her son faltered in his faithfulness, we can look to Bathsheba as an example of a redeemed mother whose broken heart God restored, and whose wisdom and virtuous character began with her obedience to God, even in the midst of sorrow.

THE WOMANHOOD OF BATHSHEBA

Although her story in the Bible begins with several instances of heartbreak after King David's sinful act, Bathsheba emerges as a true queen. Her grace, humility, loyalty, and noble character position her as a trusted voice to kings. Bathsheba faithfully honors the men in her life, including her first husband Uriah, whose death she properly mourns before moving on to becoming queen. And despite her son Solomon's eventual wayward path as king, Bathsheba's wisdom in Proverbs 31, believed to be under the guise of King Lemuel's mother, still provides guidance to women today.

Bathsheba's consistent role as a guide and confidant to kings David and Solomon, despite her own personal sorrow, also reflected her faithfulness to God. In the end, the Lord placed Bathsheba in David's life and story to ensure that the succession of kingship passed to his son Solomon. Under Solomon's rule, the first temple of God was built in Israel, which housed the presence of God among his people for the first time (1 Kings 6:12-13).

Take a moment to reflect on Bathsheba's womanhood:

What similarities do you see to your own?

What character flaws does she demonstrate, and what are her redemptive qualities?

Write down your biggest takeaway about God from Bathsheba's story below:

MARY & MARTHA

Read: Matthew 26, Luke 10, John 11

When was the last time you simply sat at the feet of Jesus and listened?

It is so easy to become busy with trivial things. We give ourselves to lists, tasks, roles, and responsibilities, whether at home or in our work lives; to-do lists come naturally to most women. I'd imagine the satisfaction of checking a task off of a list on our phones today is the same kind of satisfaction that women of Jesus's day felt when they brought in a harvest, finished sewing a garment, or hosted a fellowship dinner. We'd rather be "to-do-ing" to feel a sense of accomplishment than just about anything else. Why? Because being busy gives us the feeling that we are in control. But as we learn from Martha and Mary's story, regardless of whatever we want to accomplish, we must avoid being so busy that we completely miss being fulfilled by the presence of God.

Martha means well. She's strong, smart, driven, and dedicated. A hard worker and pragmatic thinker who cares a lot about Jesus, Martha wants to make sure He is as comfortable as possible in her home. Fiercely loyal—to God and to her family—Martha appears to run the home she shares with her sister Mary and her brother Lazarus with true hospitality. She opens her home to Jesus and His disciples (Luke 10:38). But instead of enjoying Jesus's company like her sister Mary who is seated at His feet and listening to His teaching, Martha is distracted by the preparations (Luke 10:40); she is preoccupied with the "to-do" list that comes with hosting their guests.

Martha does what many of us would do when esteemed guests are coming to our homes: play hostess. She is cleaning counters, setting plates, serving drinks, ensuring everything is perfect. Martha becomes frustrated when she realizes that her sister Mary isn't helping. We can imagine the thought process: *How dare she sit at his feet and... not help? Not be in the kitchen? Not make things presentable? Not cater to the men? Not put everyone's needs before her own?* After all, Mary is a woman too! This is what society expected women to do. Martha's frustration with Mary comes from a sincere sense of duty, and perhaps with a little jealousy that Mary is able to courageously defy traditional norms whereas she may have felt bound by them. It's interesting that Jesus doesn't agree with Martha; instead, He says that Mary is the one who is right (Luke 10:42).

In this exchange Martha's behavior is so human, so familiar, so control-driven, and so indicative of the nature of woman. In her quest to steward the great responsibility of having Jesus at her home, it appeared she had forgotten who she was speaking to—Jesus Himself. She commands Him, "tell her to help me!" (Luke 10:40), as if He should bend to her will and not the other way around. Martha's friendship with Jesus is a testament to how close He often was to the women in His life and ministry. The Bible says that Jesus loved Martha and Mary and their brother Lazarus (John 11:5). The fact that Martha was comfortable enough with Jesus to demand things from

Him speaks volumes about the relationship they must have had. The way in which He lovingly corrects her also affirms His respect for all women. Jesus sees women as equals in conversation and allows them to listen in and learn from his teachings, becoming his disciples, which was an honor typically reserved for males. It's Jesus who suggests that Mary is correct in doing something radically different from traditional norms, further proving his intent to challenge the tradition and culture of the day.

Mary's devotion to Jesus is admirable, but it isn't unlike her sister's. Martha, too, is shown to be devoted to Jesus. But what made Mary different? The most striking quality that Mary displays in this moment, and also every other encounter we read that she has with Jesus, is her willingness to enter into Jesus' presence and receive His peace. While Martha is distracted by her preparations, Mary sits at the Lord's feet and listens (Luke 10:40). Jesus describes her choice as the better one. While Martha is worried and upset about many things, only one thing is needed: His presence (Luke 10:42).

Later on, when Martha and Mary's brother Lazarus dies, Martha's controlling nature exerts itself again. She takes issue with Jesus' seemingly slow arrival, suggesting that He let her brother die (John 11:21). Notice that in their exchange about what happened, Martha doesn't question whether or not Jesus can heal or resurrect Lazarus. Her faith, and their relationship, is strong enough for her to believe He is able to bring her brother back to life. She affirms that Jesus is the Messiah and capable of raising Lazarus at any time (John 11:21-27). The problem, then, was that it didn't happen when she wanted it to. Jesus didn't do it the way she wanted Him to. In saying that Jesus could have come faster, she's really saying that He should have done it her way. Without realizing it, Martha tries to tell Jesus what He should have done. Crazy, right? But we women do this all the time. We often want to take control of the situation and solve a problem in our lives with a plan we devise. Anything else would require us to have patience, be still, trust

God and listen. It would require us to sit at the feet of Jesus or wait for His instruction. To do that, Martha would have to be more like her sister Mary.

When Lazarus died, Mary was equally upset. But while Martha rushes out to meet Jesus when He finally comes to Bethany, Mary instead waits in the house for Jesus to call her into His presence (John 11:28). As soon as He calls, she comes quickly (John 11:29). She also asserts her faith in the Lord and His ability to prevent Lazarus from dying if He were there, but she is so overcome with emotion in the moment that it moves the Lord to weep Himself (John 11:35). His compassion for his friends and their loss, despite knowing that He is going to raise Lazarus from the dead, shows how Jesus is divinely human and ever close to the brokenhearted. Indeed He will perform the miracle, but first he identifies with His people in their sorrow. This profound act of God's compassion is still His nature; He is still close to us today.

Finally, Jesus performs His last public miracle before He faces the crucifixion. Lazarus is raised to life, but not before Martha reminds us of her humanness one last time. She seemingly objects, telling Jesus that the dead body will have an odor after four days in the tomb when He asks to have the stone moved (John 11:39). To Martha's credit, she probably just didn't want to offend Him with the stench. But Jesus lovingly reminds her of her faith and to whom she spoke, *"Did I not tell you that if you believe, you will see the glory of God?" (John 11:40)*

He is still asking that of us today. Remember, Jesus told Martha that "few things are needed, indeed only one." (Luke 10:42). When in the presence of God, the concerns of the world, the details and preparations, all fade away. They aren't important. His glory is present. And in that environment, the impossible is possible.

THE WOMANHOOD OF MARY & MARTHA

The lives of these two sisters in just two quick exchanges tell us more about God's relationship with those He loves than many other stories in the Bible. Mary and Martha (and their brother Lazarus) are loved by Jesus—close enough for Him to call them friends, comfortable enough for them to host His presence in their home, and dear enough to His heart for Him to weep compassionately in their time of sorrow. Martha means well when she complains to him; although in her grumbling she exerts the controlling nature of women, she never questions his deity. Her feminine urge to dominate circumstances and situations, and in many ways tell God what to do, is too relatable for many of us. But God is patient with us, and Jesus honors our humanness, just as He did with Martha. Jesus may have scolded Martha, but he never rebuked her. Instead, He points out Mary's response and urges us all to have the same heart posture of rest in His presence.

Take a moment to reflect on Mary and Martha's womanhood:

What similarities do you see to your own?

What character flaws do they each demonstrate, and what are their redemptive qualities?

Write down your biggest takeaway about God from Mary and Martha's story below:

THE WOMAN AT THE WELL

Read: John 4

How do you know that you are seen and known by God?

One encounter with Jesus can change everything. The Woman at the Well experienced this; her life transformed so significantly and profoundly that by the end of it she had to run and tell everyone in town to "come and see." For such a quick passage in John 4, the story of the woman at the well is one that resonates throughout history for its beauty. The story of a less-than-perfect woman who meets a perfect Savior tells us a lot about His desire for everyone to come to know Him just as intimately. Bringing our murky pasts, our hard truths, and our unsatisfied hearts to His presence, we can receive freedom, love, and unspeakable joy that can't be contained—it must be shared with others. This is the God who revealed Himself as Messiah to a Samaritan woman that day.

The unnamed woman's story in John 4 begins with the acknowledgement of Jesus's passage through Samaria on his way to Galilee (John 4:1). To avoid the Pharisees and their attempts to call him out for baptizing people, he takes a longer route than He needs in order to meet this woman. Of course, Jesus knows the reputation that Samaritans have, which explains the woman's surprise when He asks her for a drink (John 4:8). Historically, Jews despised Samaritans because they were mixed-race people. Half Jewish and half Gentile, the Samaritans were descendants of foreigners who resettled and intermarried with the remaining Jews in Israel after the Assyrians conquered the land and exiled the majority (Nelson, 2009). These Gentiles brought with them pagan idols and practices, different political beliefs, and a loose understanding of the Torah that the Jews held so dear.

Interestingly, their Jewish ancestry connected Samaritans to Joseph, the one son who was hated and cast out by the other eleven sons of Jacob, the patriarchs of the tribes of Israel. With Jacob's blessing of fruitfulness to his favorite son Joseph (Genesis 49:22), the land allotted to Joseph's sons Manasseh and Ephraim eventually became the flourishing region of Samaria. Centuries later, Jesus meets the Samaritan woman, who is a representation of His kingdom of Jews and Gentiles together, in this same place by Jacob's Well.

Jesus breaks several traditional norms and behaviors by speaking to the woman at the well, revealing His character and His heart. Not only does he speak to a Samaritan, he speaks to a Samaritan woman, which is completely out of character for a Jewish man. Moreover, He spoke to a Samaritan woman who was an outcast from even her own society. Her reputation as a woman with several ex-husbands, currently living with a man she was not married to, made her a pariah. They both meet at the well at high noon in order to avoid people. He was weary from avoiding the Pharisees; she wanted to avoid the mockery and stares of the other women of the town who gossiped about her, which Jesus directly addressed in their exchange.

He starts with a request, "will you give me a drink" (John 4:7), which begins their conversation about living water. Jesus offered living water as a symbol of eternal life and freedom (John 4:13-14). He reveals his intention to see beyond her past or current circumstances when He offers her spiritual water—everlasting love and acceptance. The physical water from the well would inevitably run out; on the contrary, the spiritual water Jesus offers needs no refilling. The Samaritan woman is curious and ready to accept it.

The Samaritan woman was interested in this living water because it offered a better life than the one she was currently experiencing. Without revealing her circumstances, she tells Jesus to give her the living water so that she wouldn't thirst again and wouldn't have to keep coming to Jacob's Well (John 4:15). Coming to the well meant interacting with a society that shunned her—one that judged her and called her unworthy. Jesus knew this already. He revealed the depth of His knowledge of the woman by asking her to call her husband (John 4:16). When she admitted to not having a husband, Jesus affirmed her by bringing up the intimate details of her life: that she had five husbands prior to the man she currently lived with (John 4:17-18). Although Jesus spoke directly to her shame, he did so in a way that neither judged nor condemned her. Instead, he saw her heart and called her truthful.

The Woman at the Well is most often misunderstood as a prostitute or loose woman because of what we've been taught it means to be a woman associated with multiple men. However, it's important to take the culture and context of the time into consideration. A woman in first century Jewish (or Samaritan) society who had five husbands was a woman who had five legal marriages and at least four legal divorces. The Bible does not tell us what happened to each of her ex-husbands, but scholars believe that either they initiated the divorces for a specific reason (like infertility) or they had died, and thus she was legally free of those covenants (Glahn, 2024). It's unlikely that men in that day and society would have chosen to marry an adulterous woman, especially one that had so many past husbands. It's possible that she had an unfortunate combination of husbands who died, marriages that failed, possibly infertility, or even a concubine or servitude arrangement that resulted in her living with a man without being legally married to him. Whatever it was, Jesus did not judge—he simply acknowledged her truth.

We also learn a little about the woman's character in her response to the shocking revelation. Once she heard Jesus speak her truth, rather than focusing further on her personal life or seeking more knowledge from this perceived prophet, she instead asks Him a theological question: are the Jews right for the way they worship, or are the Samaritans (John 4:19-20)? This remarkable question suggested that faith was extremely important to the woman at the well. She cared deeply about the things of God, and she understood that if this was a man who knew her truth, then He must know the truth *about everything.*

Jesus took her profound question as an opportunity to reveal himself to the woman. He proclaimed that it is time for true worshippers to worship in spirit and in truth, for God is spirit and requires worship in truth (John 4:23-24). When she added that the Samaritans believed that the Messiah would come to explain everything, He helped her see that this was exactly what he was doing in their conversation. He stated that He is the Messiah (John 4:26), which marks His most explicit affirmation of His divinity recorded in the Bible. Jesus explained that He is the truth and He is the living water—the savior that eternally connects us to the Spirit of God.

The woman's encounter with Jesus at the well was so profound and transformational that she dropped her water pot and immediately ran into town to tell people about Him. "Could this be the Messiah?" she asked (John 4:29). The excitement and urgency in her actions spoke to how immensely her faith had grown in that one exchange with Jesus. Not only did He reveal truths to her that no one else would know, but He also offered her respite from the burdens that she carried in her heart. Living water would never make her thirst for the affection of man ever again.

It's amazing that the woman wanted to share her testimony and help others discover their freedom, especially because they were the same people who condemned her for her past. That is exactly the effect that Jesus can have on our lives. No longer are the things of this world important; no longer do the opinions of men matter. Jesus offers a love so deep and so secure that there is no threat to it. And it's a love worth sharing so others may also find freedom.

The actions of the woman at the well shows us her heart. She may have been broken by her life experiences, but her love of others had not grown cold. While the woman ran to share her testimony, Jesus focused His disciples on the work that He came to do, speaking to the "food" of doing the work that His Father sent Him to do (John 4:34). He uses the analogy of fields being ripe for harvest to illustrate that His work is to bring people into the Kingdom of God (John 4:35). It just so happened to be the work that the woman was doing at that very moment.

It's no coincidence that Jesus chose to go out of his way to Samaria just to encounter this particular woman at the well. He saw her heart, broken many times, but craving truth and acceptance. Her devotion to her faith and theological curiosity about the worship of Jews and Samaritans spoke to her eagerness to worship God properly. She sought to know truth, and He found her. And from this single encounter at the well, many Samaritans became believers (John 4:39-42).

How fortunate the woman was to encounter this man—the One who knew everything about her without her saying a word, who offered her a "living water" that was better than any well water she could drink. After one encounter with Him, the woman was never thirsty again.

THE WOMANHOOD OF THE WOMAN AT THE WELL

While one of the most popular stories of the women in the Bible, the Woman at the Well is gravely misunderstood. Her circumstances are often misrepresented as the result of adulterous or loose behavior, when in reality she carried the pain of heartbreak, rejection, loss, and possibly even infertility. She encounters Jesus with the heart posture of humility and a deep willingness to live a better life. She displays incredible faith when confronted with the truth. After her encounter with Jesus, she immediately becomes an evangelist, overcoming her previous rejection by society with His salvation and her testimony. The woman at the well reminds us all that Jesus is the only one that can satisfy our deepest needs with His living water. His love, grace and acceptance transcend all else. Neither marriage, nor societal acceptance or even religion could do what He did for her in an instant at the well.

Take a moment to reflect on the womanhood of the Woman at the Well:

What similarities do you see to your own?

What character flaws does she demonstrate, and what are her redemptive qualities?

Write down your biggest takeaway about God from the Woman at the Well's story below:

HIS HEART FOR US

Is it possible to know God but never truly know Him?

Think of the superficial relationships we sometimes have with other people. For example, we can live next door to a neighbor for years and never know much about them. Even if we are friendly with this neighbor and wave or say hello in passing, it does not mean we know them. Rather, we can have an idea of who they are based on these limited interactions, and then we imagine the rest. In the same way, it is possible to read Scripture without seeking to know God; without going deeper, and asking for wisdom to understand what He is trying to communicate about Himself and His will. Of course, we can never know all of God. His thoughts are higher than our thoughts, and His ways are far beyond anything we could imagine (Isaiah 55:8-9). The real takeaway from reading about the women of the Bible is to discover the aspects of God's nature that He has revealed to us in each story, and to see that His nature is unchanged.

From these stories we see that God desires for women to know Him. The Creator of the universe seeks a close and personal relationship with His beautiful creation. God's pursuit of each woman's heart is evident in each conflict or personal struggle, with the outcome requiring a choice: either she receives freedom by faith in Him, or she remains bound by hopeless circumstances that often end in death or defeat. What if Esther chose to stay silent? What if Ruth stayed in Moab? Each woman chooses to move forward in faith. God's heart posture is a willingness to draw near to those who draw near to Him (James 4:8) and change their lives for the better.

From Eve, Rahab, and the Woman at the Well, we learn that God is not looking for perfection. Despite our sinfulness, his faithfulness endures. So, for the woman who feels ashamed of her past or bound by a reputation that feels inescapable, take heart—God offers freedom and protection in Him.

Bathsheba and Esther show us the courage it takes to lead, even in the midst of conflict or sorrow, with a heart posture of humility and submission to God. For the woman who feels called to a position of prominence but doubts her qualifications, rest assured that in Him, there is no imposter syndrome. God calls His daughters to queenship and equips us for the palace.

God wants us to have sisterhood, which we can learn from the stories of Rachel and Leah and Ruth and Naomi. Sisterhood is not found in jealousy and competition, but is found in loyalty and love. It requires humility that enables us to lean on each other in times of trouble and fervent faith that carries us through all seasons. If you have never seen another woman as your sister, it's not too late. Sisterhood has kingdom-building purpose, and God honors women who commit to strengthening each other in faith.

We see in the examples of Sarah, Hagar, Mary, and Martha that God is the one who is in control, not us. He wants His daughters to depend fully on Him, to sit at His feet, and to rest in His finished work. To the woman questioning His promises in the midst of delay or denial, be reminded of His goodness, and submit to His perfect timing.

The women of the Bible and their stories of triumph reflect the victory and redemption found in our Savior, Jesus Christ. In Him we are protected and cared for, secure in God's love, and given the blessed assurance of a personal, enduring relationship with Him. There is rest in this: if we have Jesus, we have everything we need for our womanhood to flourish.

As we study the lives of the women of the Bible, finding similarities to our own lives and taking note of their mistakes, may we find that God's heart toward women is enduring—He still calls us suitable helpmates, worthy daughters, queens, and His beloved creation.

WORKS CITED

Baker, R. (2020, May 29). *Reclaiming and Re-affirming Biblical Sisterhood.* The Gospel Coalition | Australia. https://au.thegospelcoalition.org/article/reclaiming-and-re-affirming-biblical-sisterhood/

Bonesteele, Y. (2022, March 23). *Our Invisible Scarlet Cord.* The Gospel Project. https://gospelproject.lifeway.com/our-invisible-scarlet-cord/

Eames, C. (2024, June 7). *Was Rahab Really a Canaanite?* Armstrong Institute of Biblical Archaeology. https://armstronginstitute.org/1056-was-rahab-really-a-canaanite

Glahn, S. L. (2024, March 22). *The "Woman at the Well": Was the Samaritan Woman Really an Adulteress? | Biblical Studies.* Kregel Academic and Ministry. https://kregelacademicblog.com/biblical-studies/the-woman-at-the-well-was-the-samaritan-woman-really-an-adulteress/

Got Questions Ministries. (2022, January 4). *Why did Queen Vashti refuse to appear before Xerxes?* Got Questions. https://www.gotquestions.org/Vashti-Xerxes.html

Kadari, T. (2009, March 20). *Rachel: Midrash and Aggadah.* Shalvi/Hyman Encyclopedia of Jewish Women. https://jwa.org/encyclopedia/article/rachel-midrash-and-aggadah#pid-16553

Mackie, T., & Sullivan, A. (2017, March 4). *Joshua: Judgment or Cruelty? Conquering the Promised Land.* The Bible Project. https://bibleproject.com/articles/judgement-cruelty-conquering-promised-land/

Nelson, T. (2009, February 2). *Hatred Between Jews and Samaritans.* Bible.org. Retrieved January 30, 2026, from https://bible.org/illustration/hatred-between-jews-and-samaritans

Ophoff, G. M. (1942, May 15). The Place of the Book of Esther in the Canon. *The Standard Bearer*, *18*(16). https://sb.rfpa.org/the-place-of-the-book-of-esther-in-the-canon/

Rendsburg, G. A. (2021). *Woman: Helpmate No Longer.* The Torah. https://www.thetorah.com/article/woman-helpmate-no-longer

Richardson, A. (2018, June 29). *Bathsheba Was Not on the Roof: And Here's Why That Is Important.* On Sovereign Wings. https://onsovereignwings.wordpress.com/2018/06/29/bathsheba-wasnt-on-the-roof-and-heres-why-that-is-important/

Robinson, M. (1993, February/March). *Ruth and Boaz: The Story of the Kinsman-Redeemer – Israel My Glory.* Israel My Glory. https://israelmyglory.org/article/ruth-and-boaz-the-story-of-the-kinsman-redeemer/

Schnorr, J. (2024, December 20). *30 Bible Verses on Women Leading.* Marg Mowczko. Retrieved January 28, 2026, from https://margmowczko.com/bible-verses-on-women-leaders/

Smith, T. (2026). *Ruth 3:4 Uncovering his feet.* St. Paul's Lutheran Church. https://splnewulm.org/devotions/ruth-34-uncovering-his-feet/

ABOUT THE AUTHOR

CHIDERAH COX is an author, worship leader, and Bible teacher based in the Washington, D.C. metropolitan area with her husband and children. She has led several book and Bible study groups for women and youth in church and at home, and often teaches about worship and biblical womanhood. Chiderah is passionate about helping women and children discover the beauty of God's Word and the truth of their identities in Christ. She has been studying the women of the Bible since 2016.

Visit **www.chiderahcox.com** to learn more about this author and browse related resources.

www.ingramcontent.com/pod-product-compliance
Lightning Source LLC
LaVergne TN
LVHW011031110826
845149LV00015B/3376

* 9 7 9 8 9 9 5 0 5 7 4 0 6 *